Love is not always
Right
But we do it any way
So in this context how
Can it ever be something which we don't want it to be
Well I will let the characters in this book
Explain that, then you can take it from there
For yourselfs.

       Statements by
  Marsha Sullivan

Chapter 1

   Look at your kiss is it the same as it was 30 days ago.
Yes, no it is not and I will call her phone to get you to tell me
about that jobeck.
Well, I love sexy woman
And you come down on me for that I can,t take it
We not married or in the moment of spice and you want to
come at me for every little touch of
Fine women that I may
Uncover. But I still got kisses for you laina. Well your lips say
this but your mind is not with my body this evening look he is
not into my smile or touch so this only means one thing I have
lost you and

It is pointless to go on but here's a kiss between our lips to so you will know that I will be your friend till the end not the lover you thought you needed good bye jobeck it was fun.

So I walk away from the table and I smile. Now I can find me a new lover and I can now regain passion y'all yes what every sexy woman is in need of pure new relationship with no lacking in desire. So now I call my stand by a sexy player by the name of Teyno. A walking painting of warrior-ness who's smile and the words which come out of his mouth have you so messed up all you can do is go right to bed with this man. Yes its weird but the only way I can explain it is his charm is a warrior taking hold of his woman in such a way that once you are into him its no going back. Lady's I will take a walk with you, and see for yourselfs and tell me that this desire of mine is not sexy and I will be amazed that you are not under his spell. Oh its that take hold look in his eyes that got me. He seem like he not even effected by what ever he does its really Something which I have

Never had in my life before. The contest was hot, even if it was 80 degree's. I was hot in all my gear waiting on this kind of lover to come and join me in a drink of

Wet water in that pool of lustful play just kissing at me as I keep hitting in the water and coming up kissing and playing with him. Oh he liked that yes he liked it so much he would not let me out the pool. So I had to confuse him by saying. Oh honey can you rub the pain out of my backside. What how can some one as sexy as you be in pain. Well I need you to

and I whispered in his ear take me in the guest house behind the pool and I will show you my pain. So he picks me up And carry's me away from everyone once he does we are alone and I get in the guest house and I smile at him and I start running from him catch me teyno. I laugh and he laughing to oh I

Will and he gives me this look like well you think that I can't get to you well then you don't know me to well. Romance and pleasure are what I do so don't be

Surprised by my Passion cause its going to make you different then you have ever been. So I smile and laugh this can not be true so once I say this he kisses me and my lips become his. He has me in his embrace and we are taking it to the next level. And we start yelling a and shaking by the passion it just surprised us. Then he says I want some more. Then he kisses me again and we going down into love making once again hot and passionate he tastes so good I just can't stand it.

Then its like 2:00am in the morning and our desire for one another was so endless. That I thought after this we would not see each other but I was wrong it

Was something else going on and lady's it was hottest when provoked by moments alone with one another. So I give him something never seen before. I twist at the touch and drop to taste all of that love which has him screaming for me to do this again but in the back of my mind I was saying can this be happening.

Chapter 2

So into the air that air I go. As I come back up and now am on top of the moment.Oh sliding down that mountain of sexy man; Slide hot and all into his chest moving and riding that moment of pleasure which turned into hours for us so sexy and hot its so unspeakable. So I can't put words to it by I can say sounds to its reachings of momentum's! So I was always ready for all this to come at me any time of the day. What ever I was doing I would stop and give this sex man what he wanted my fantasy's oh endorsed by moments with just looking him over and thinking so sexy he hot. Like a gun which has gone bang and no stopping its fire its out and I am coming without even realizing I was under his spell. I would shower and he would come in the bathroom and join me.And that always turned into a whole lot of something else.

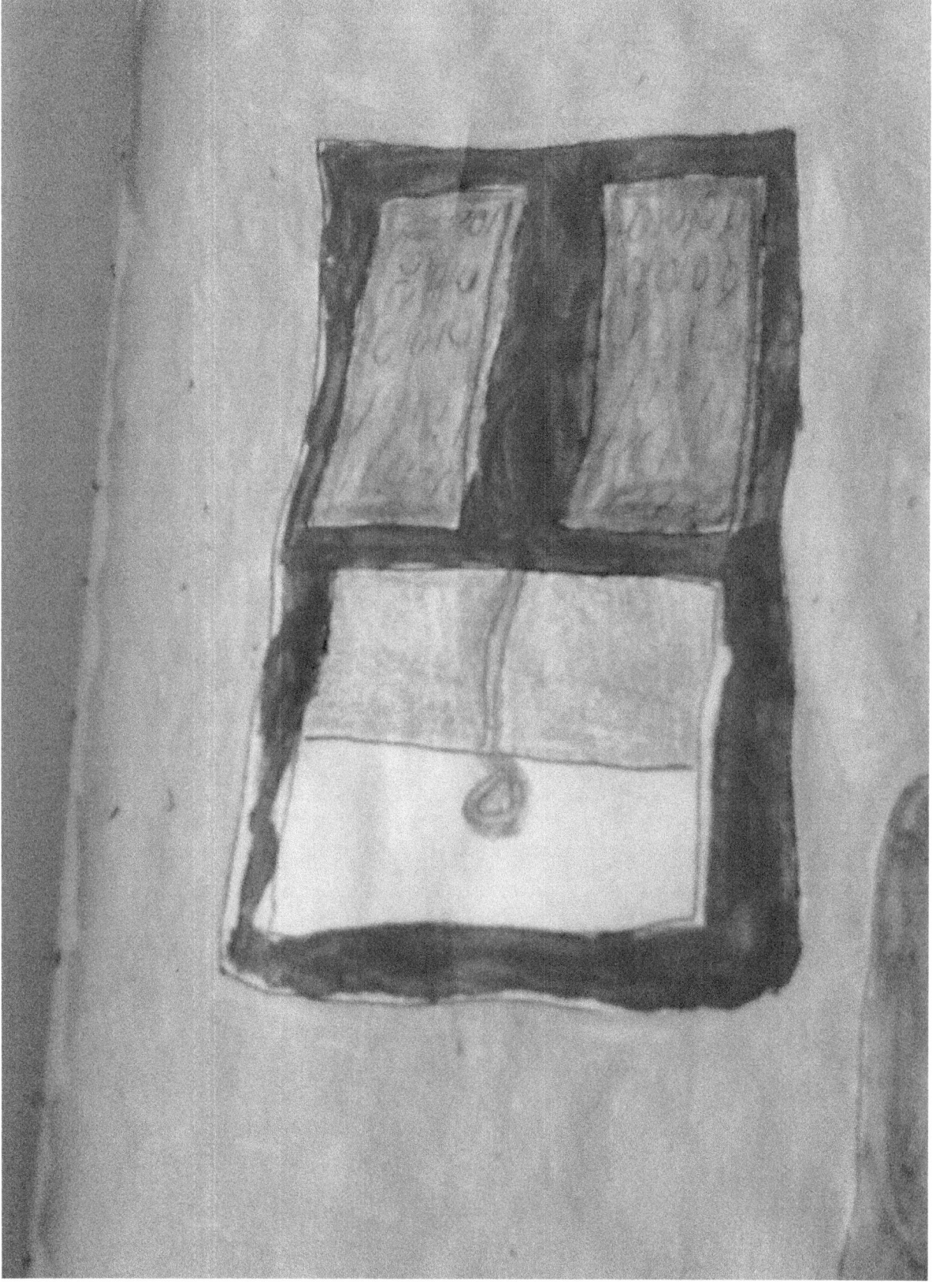

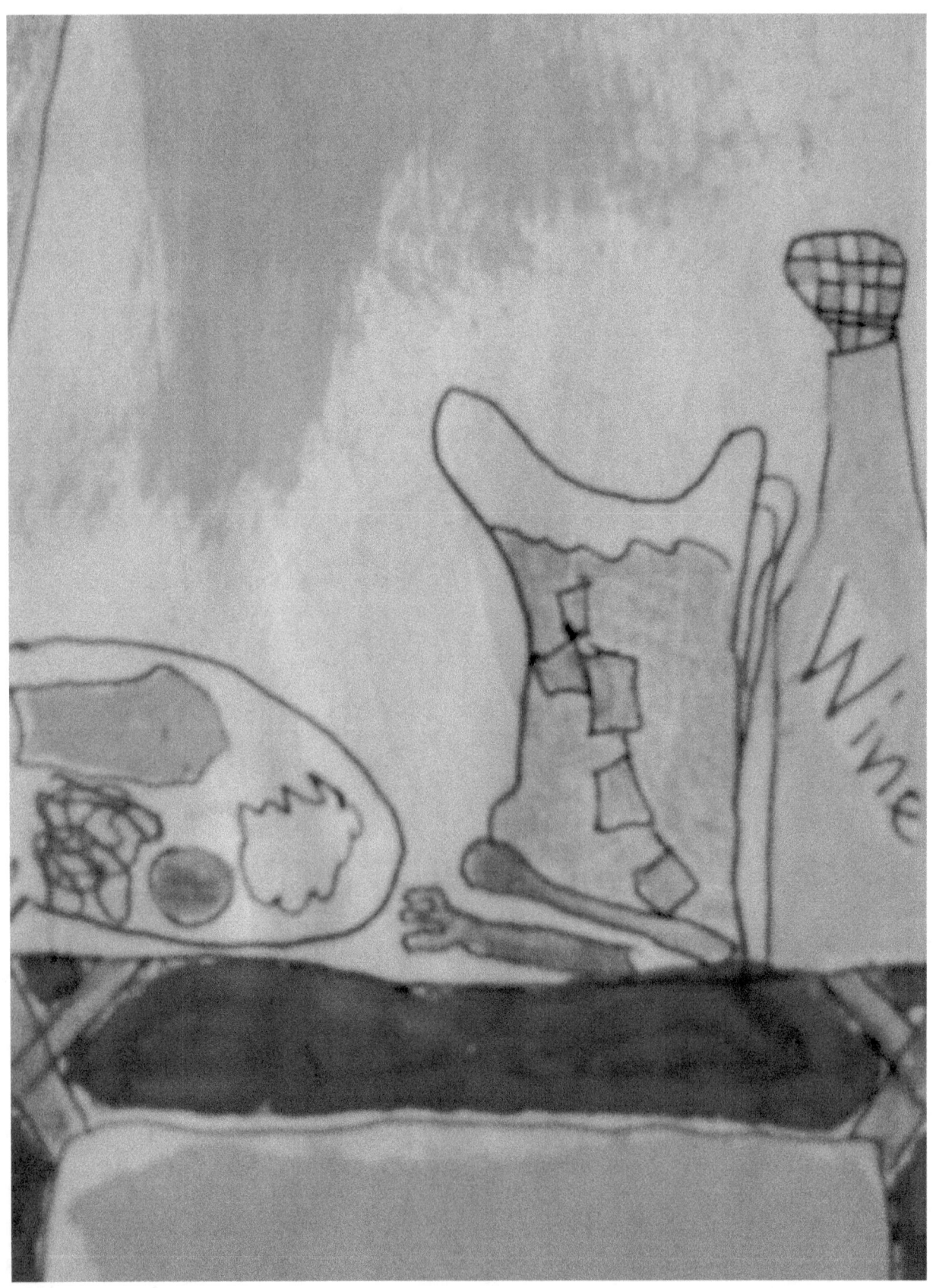

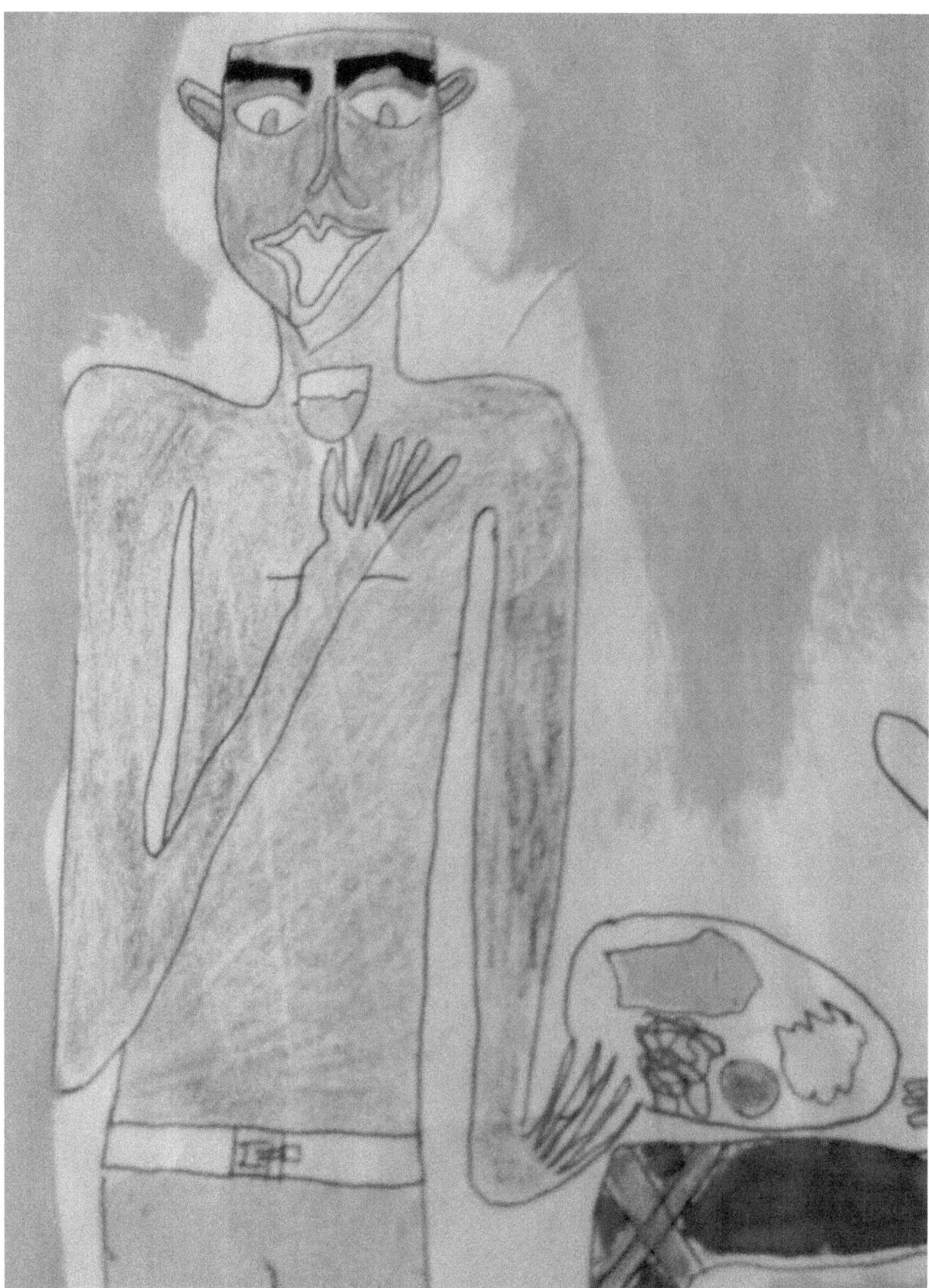

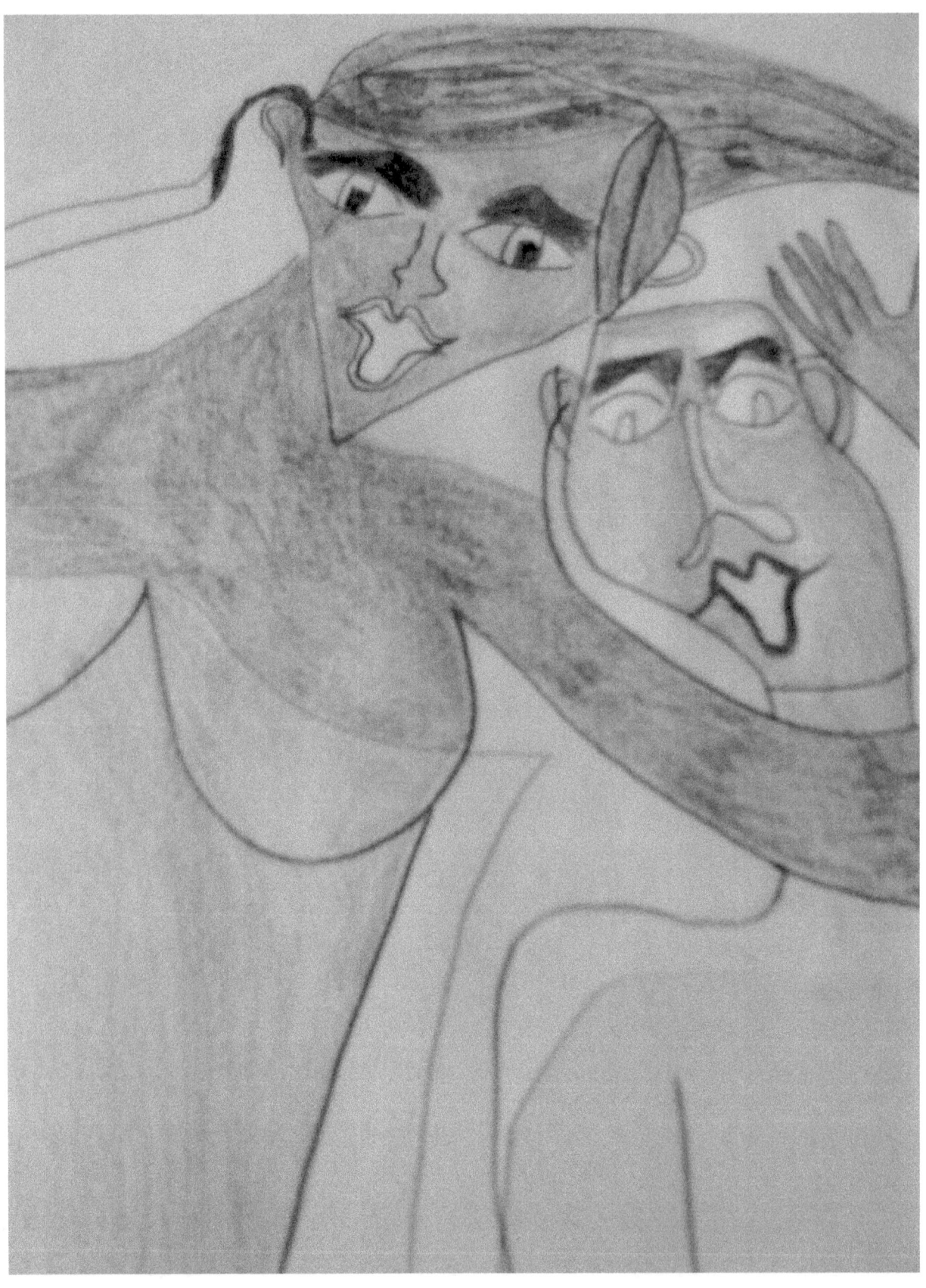

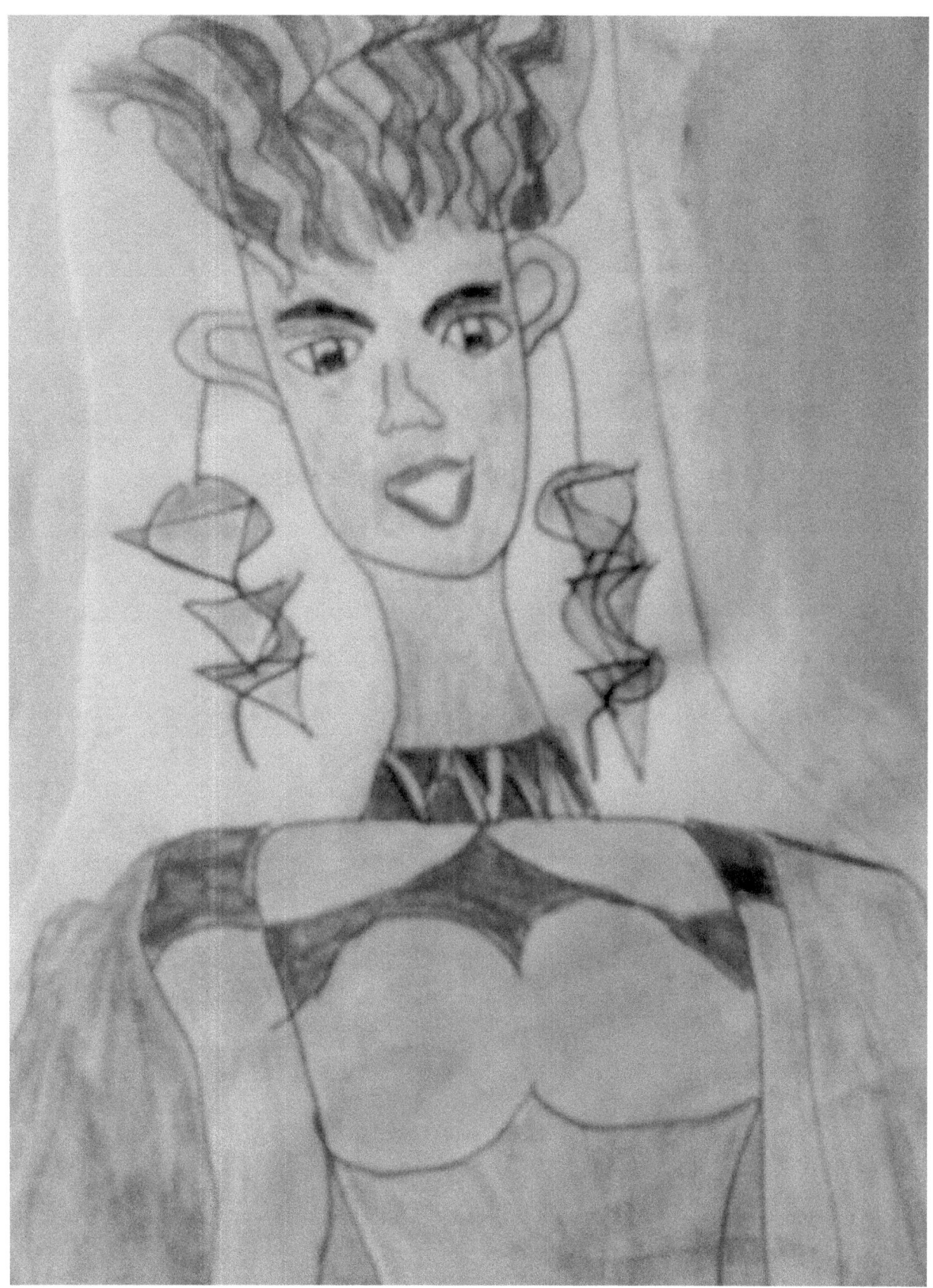

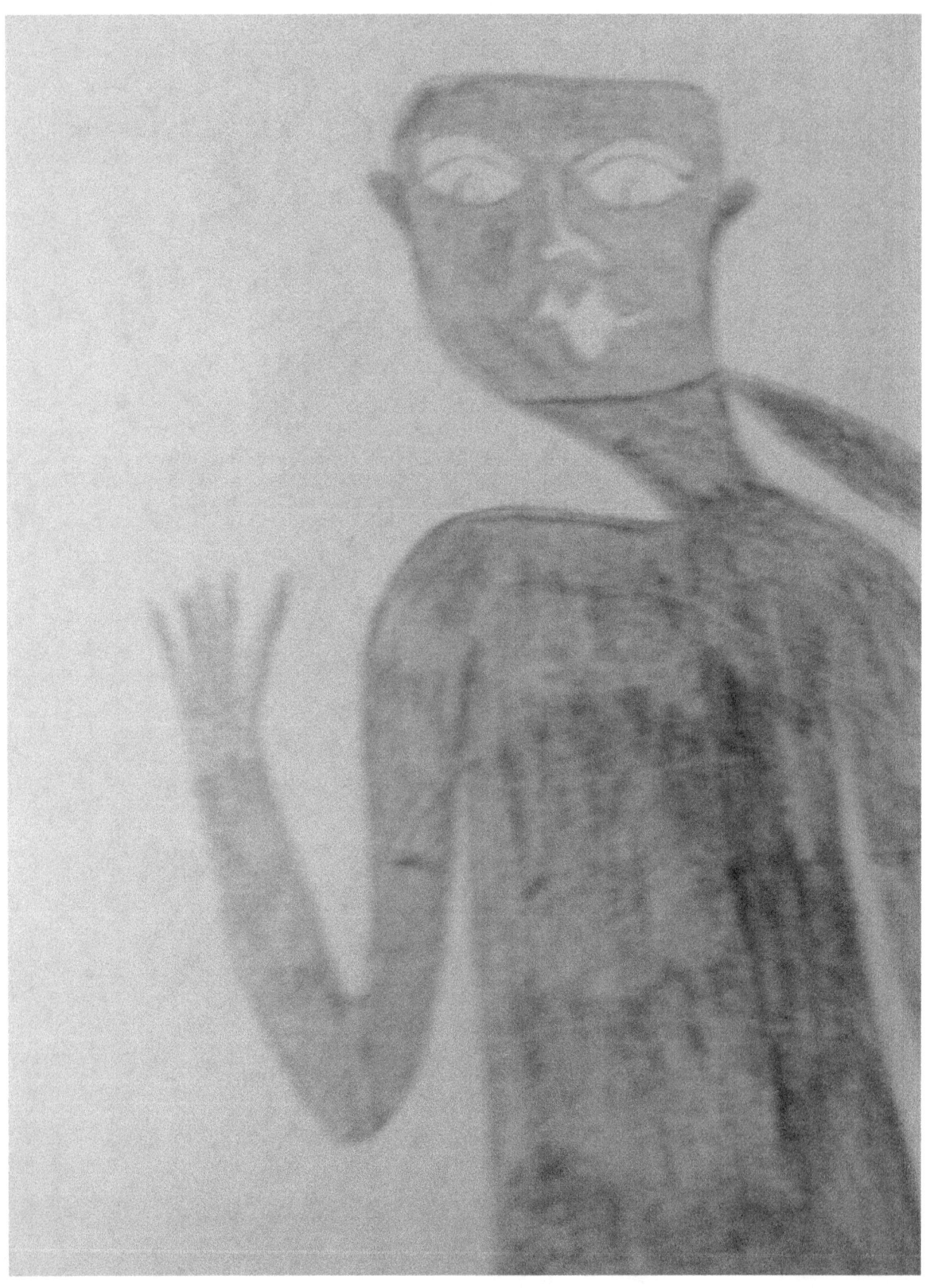

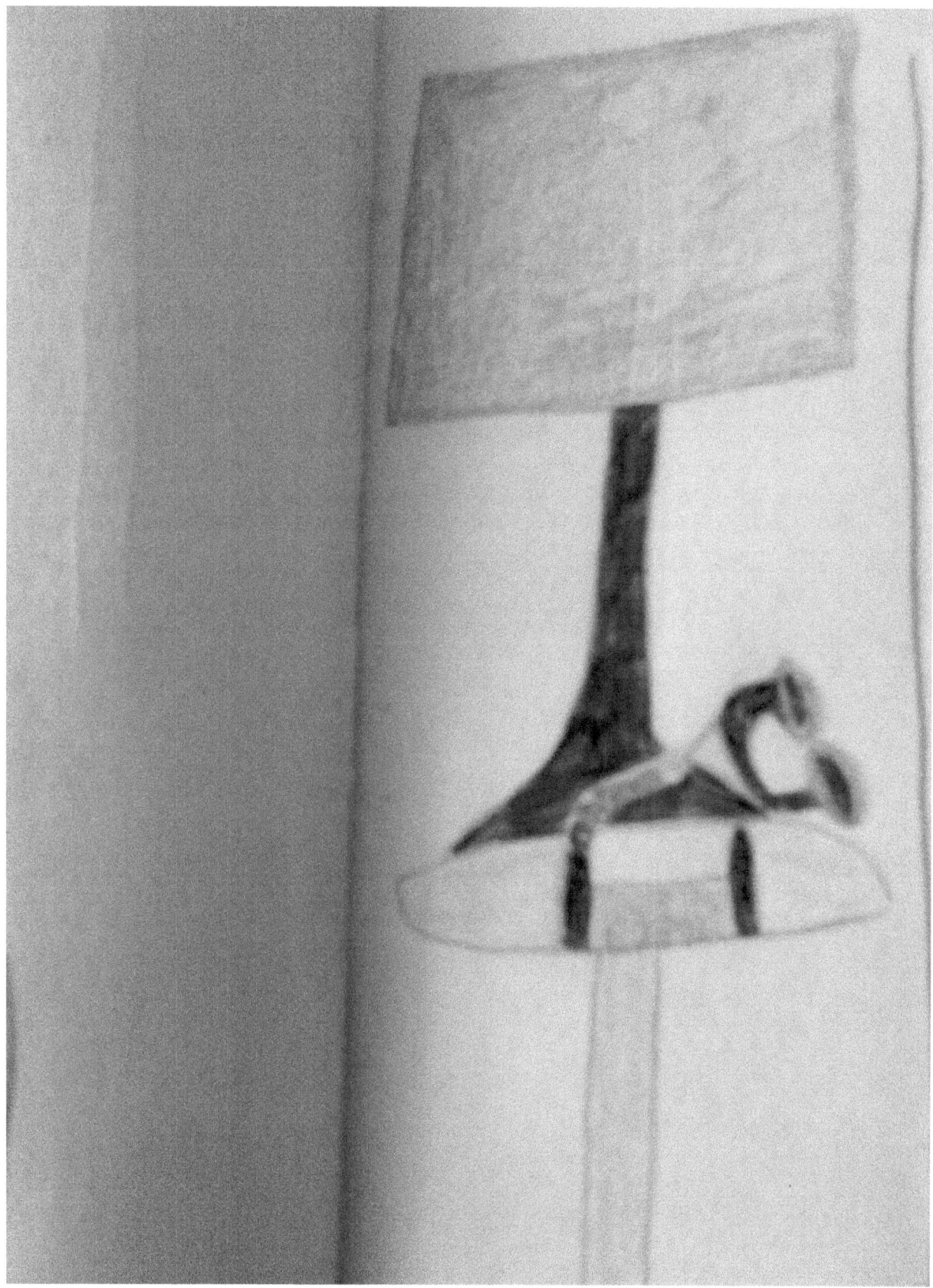

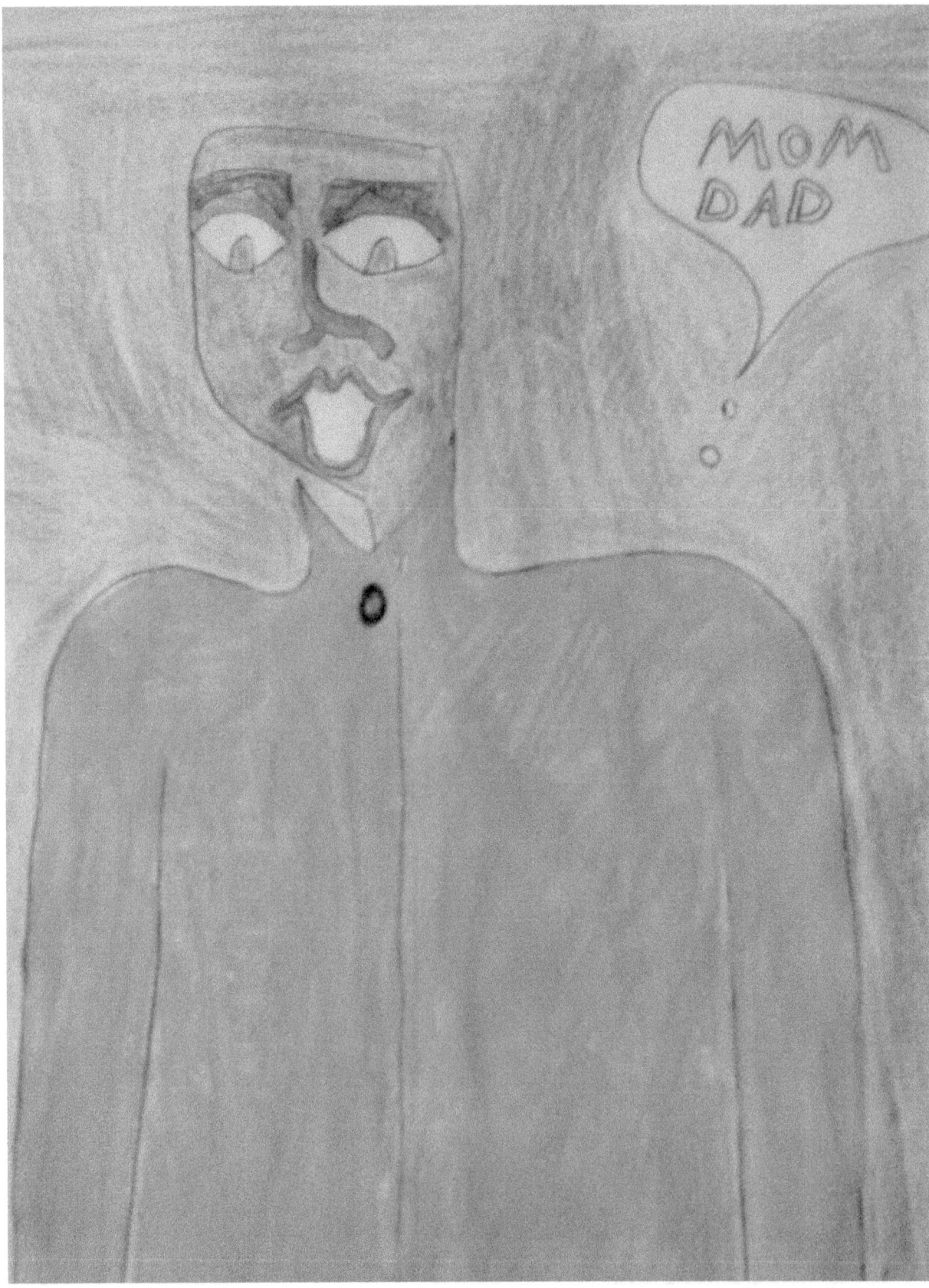

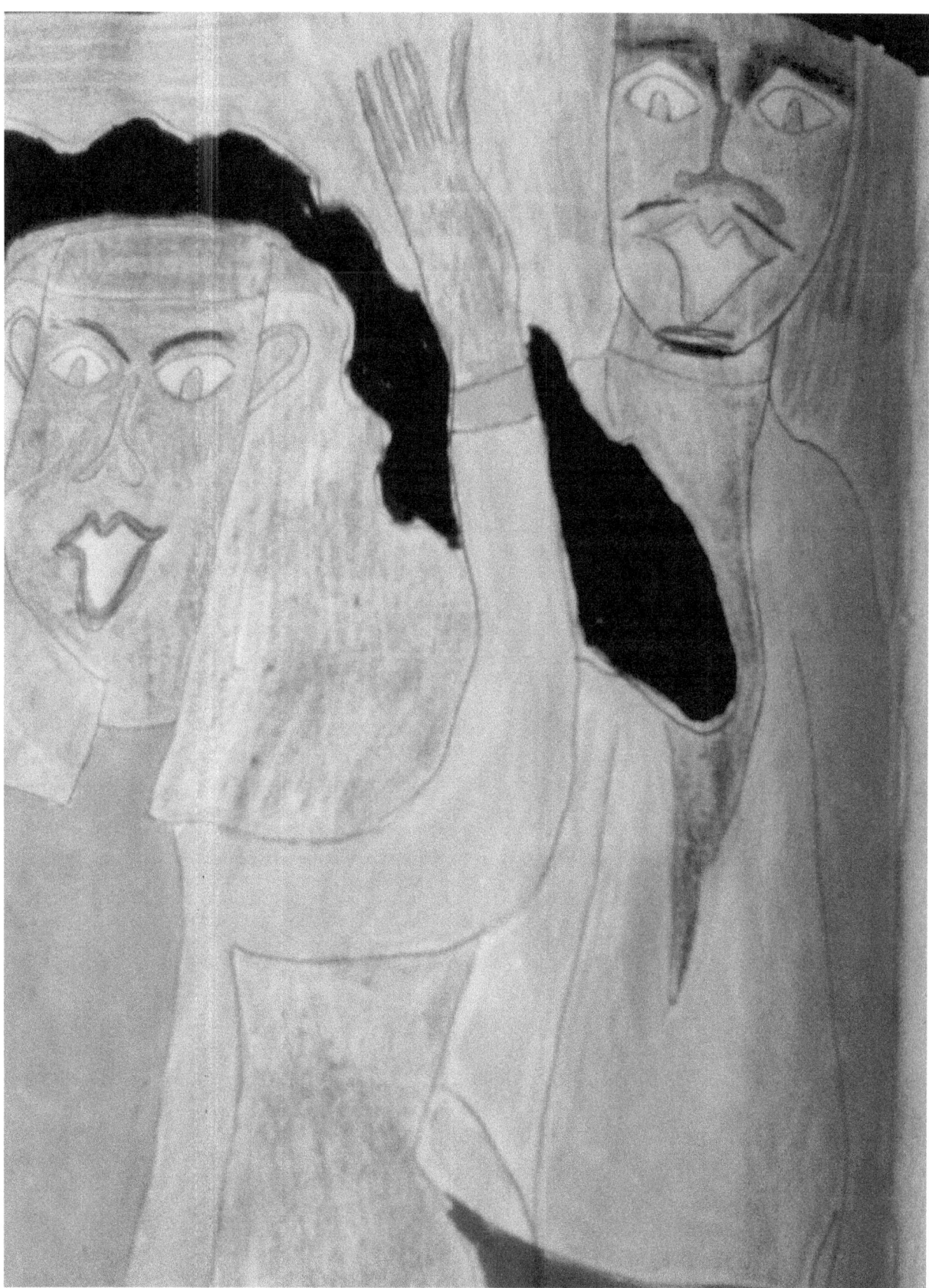

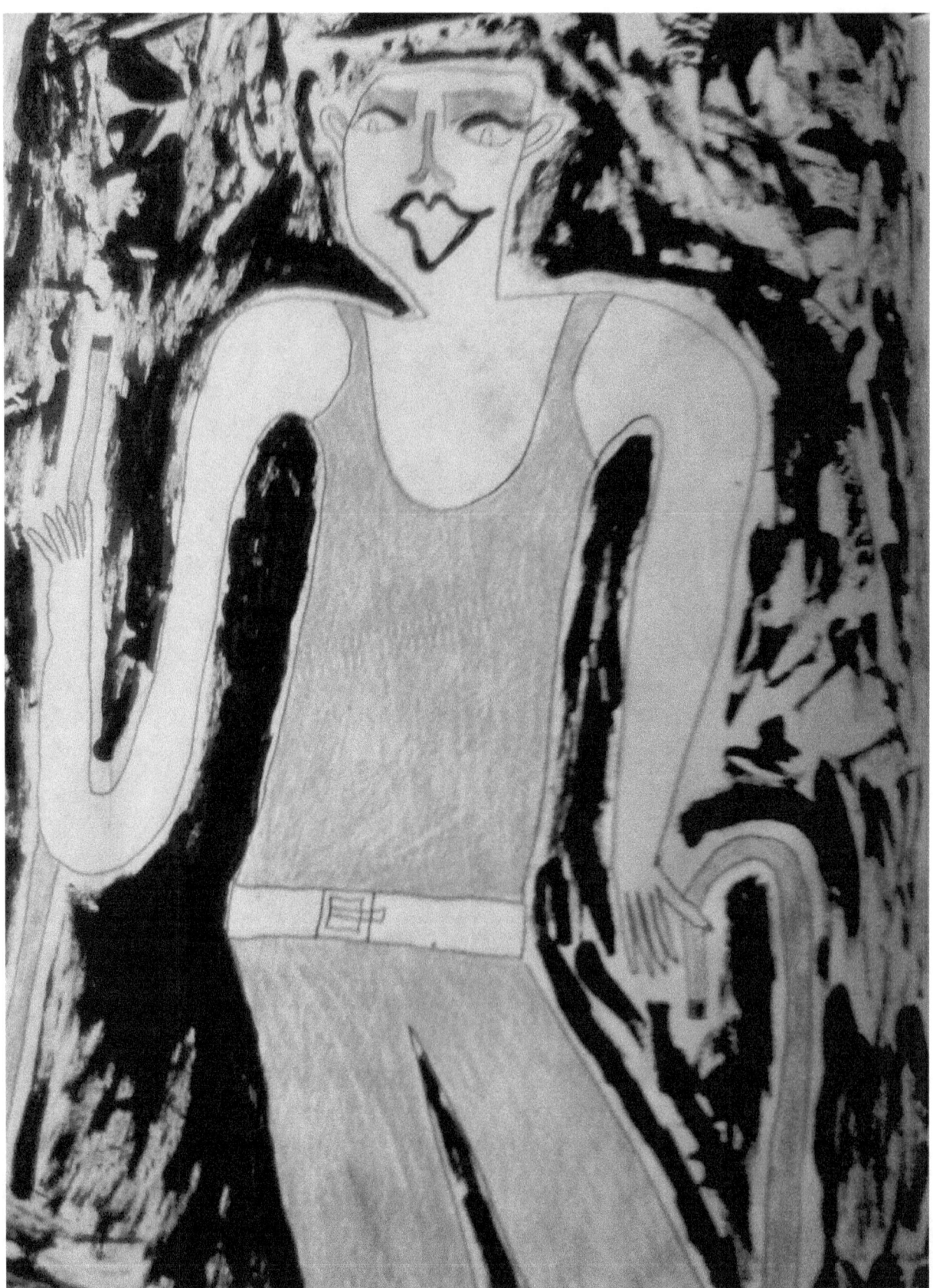

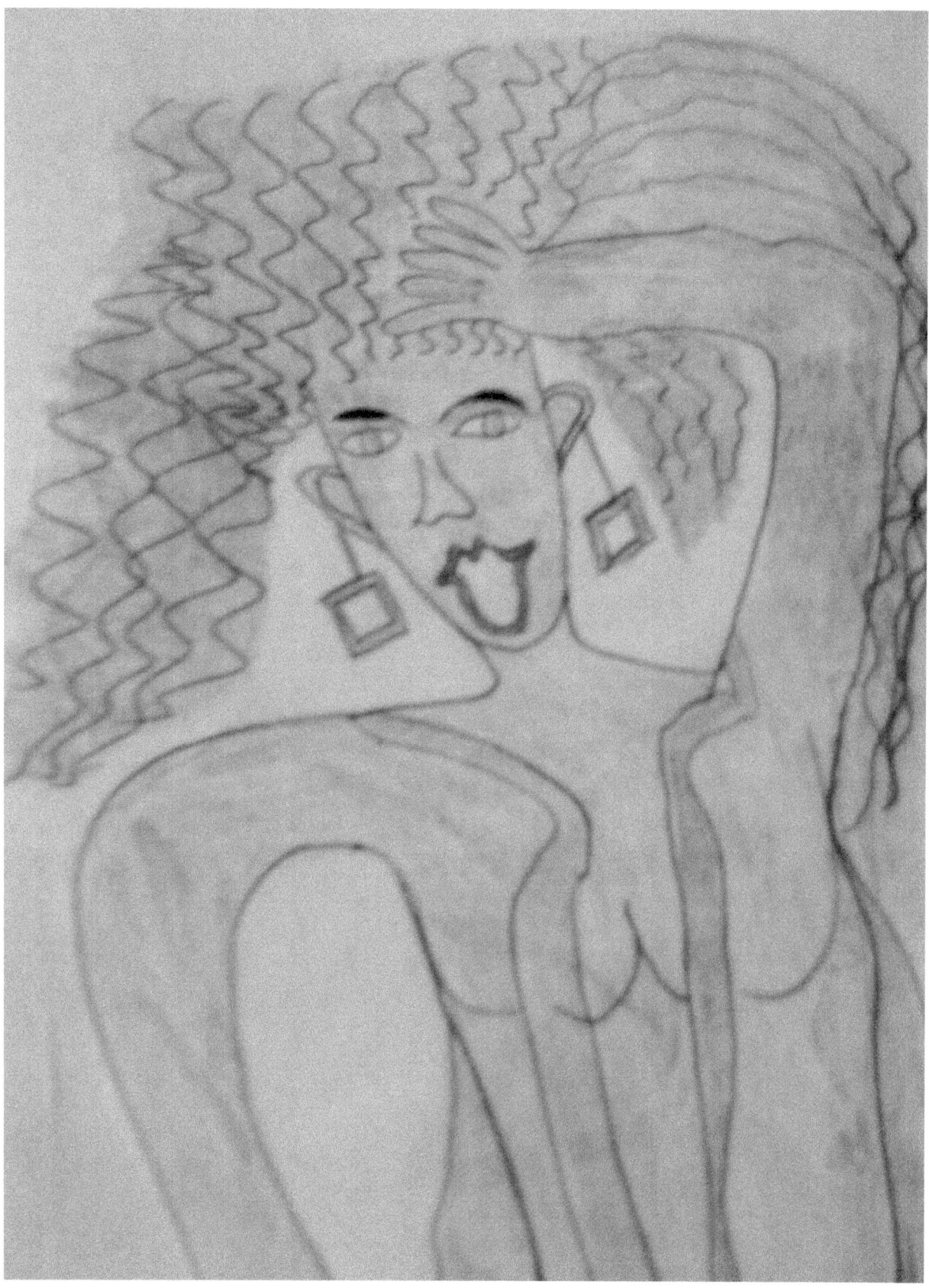

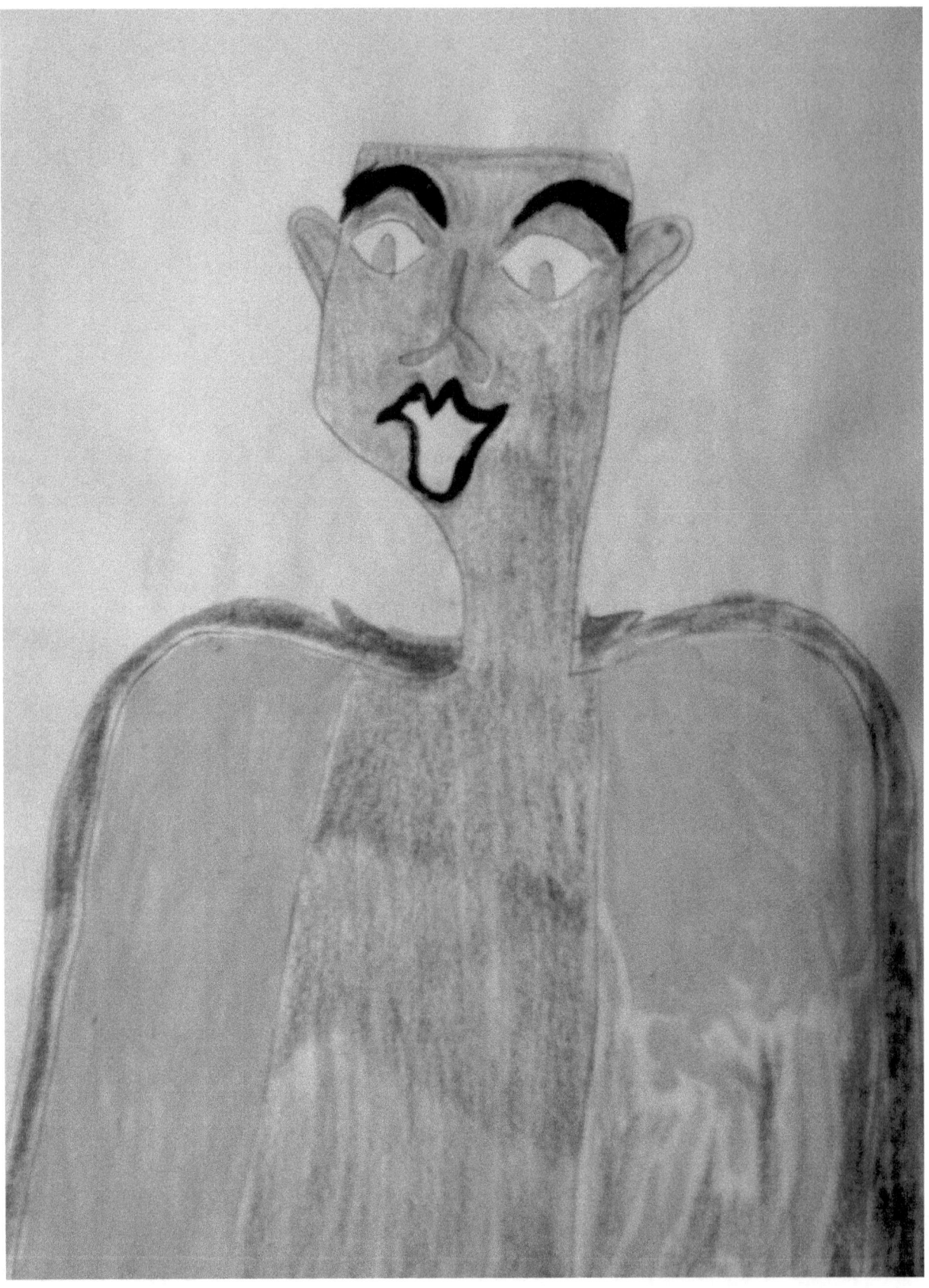

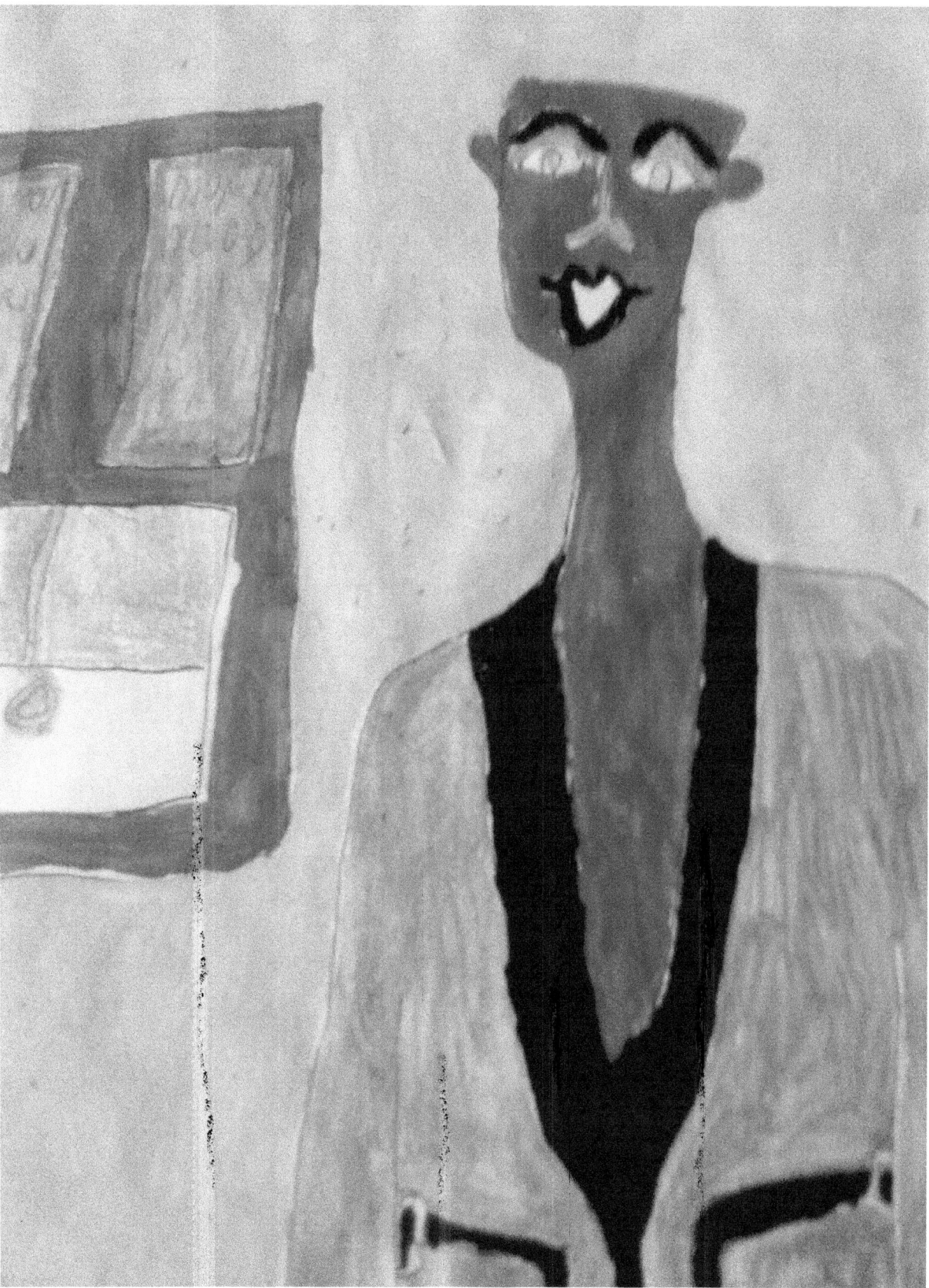

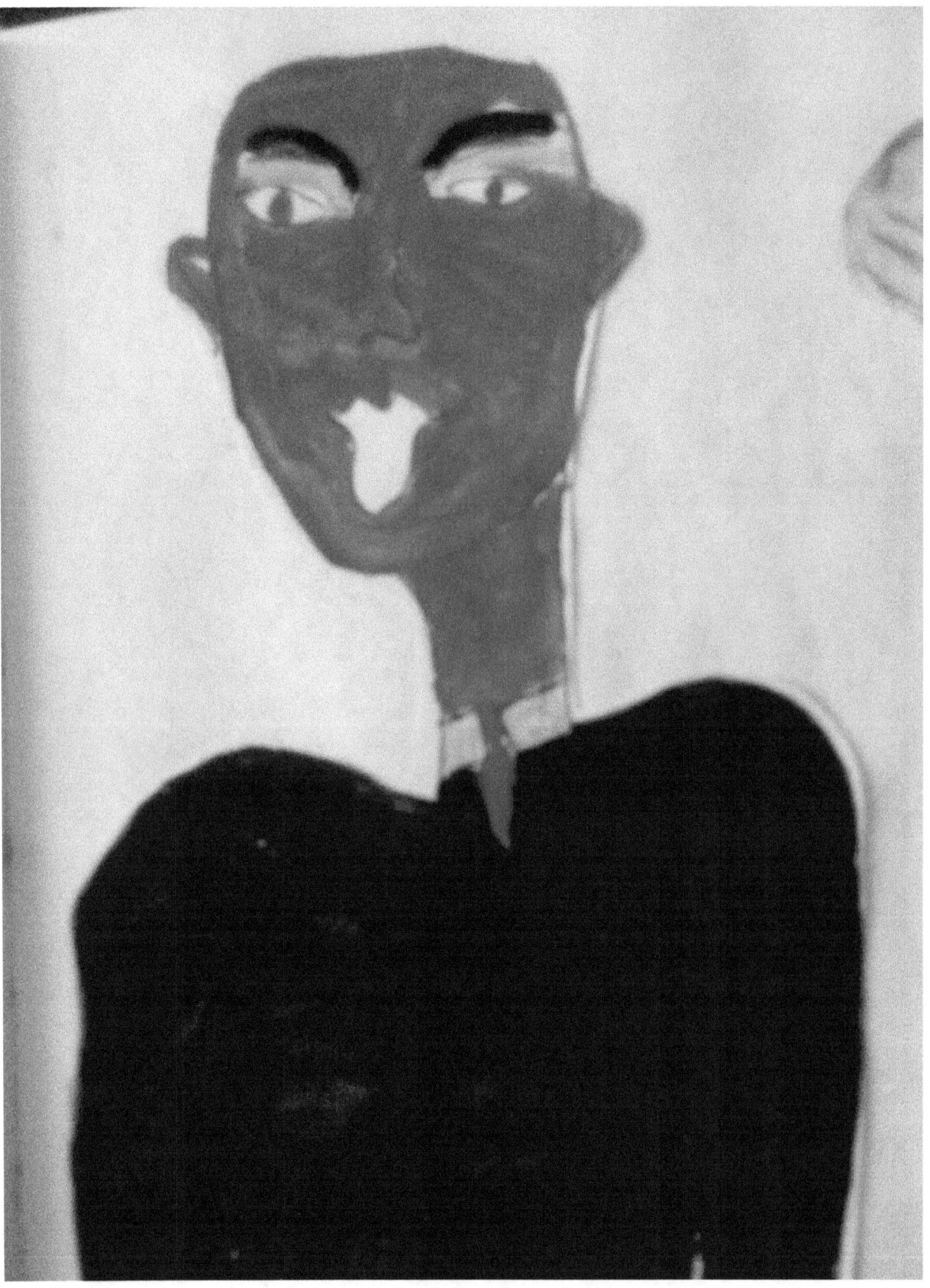

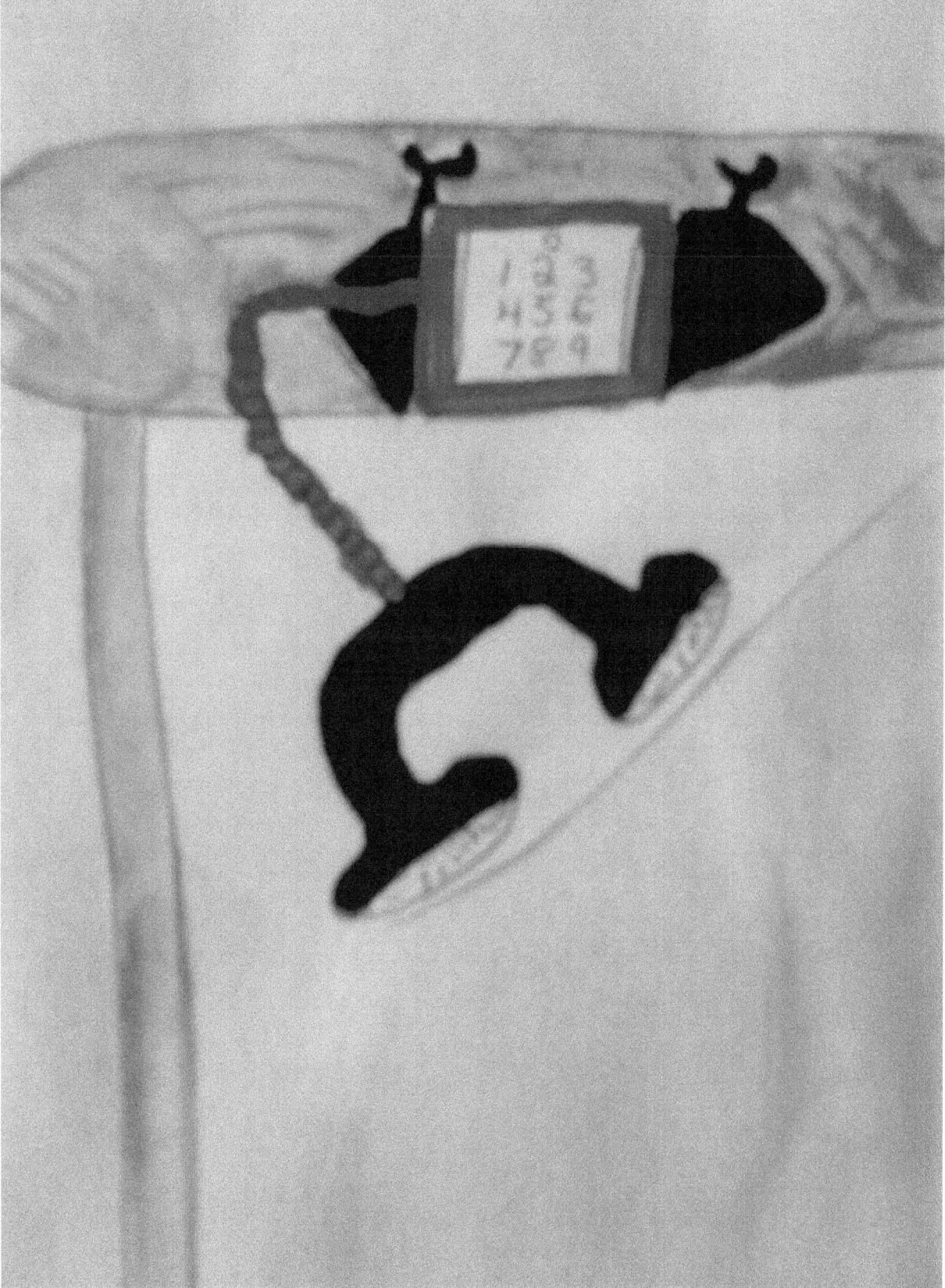

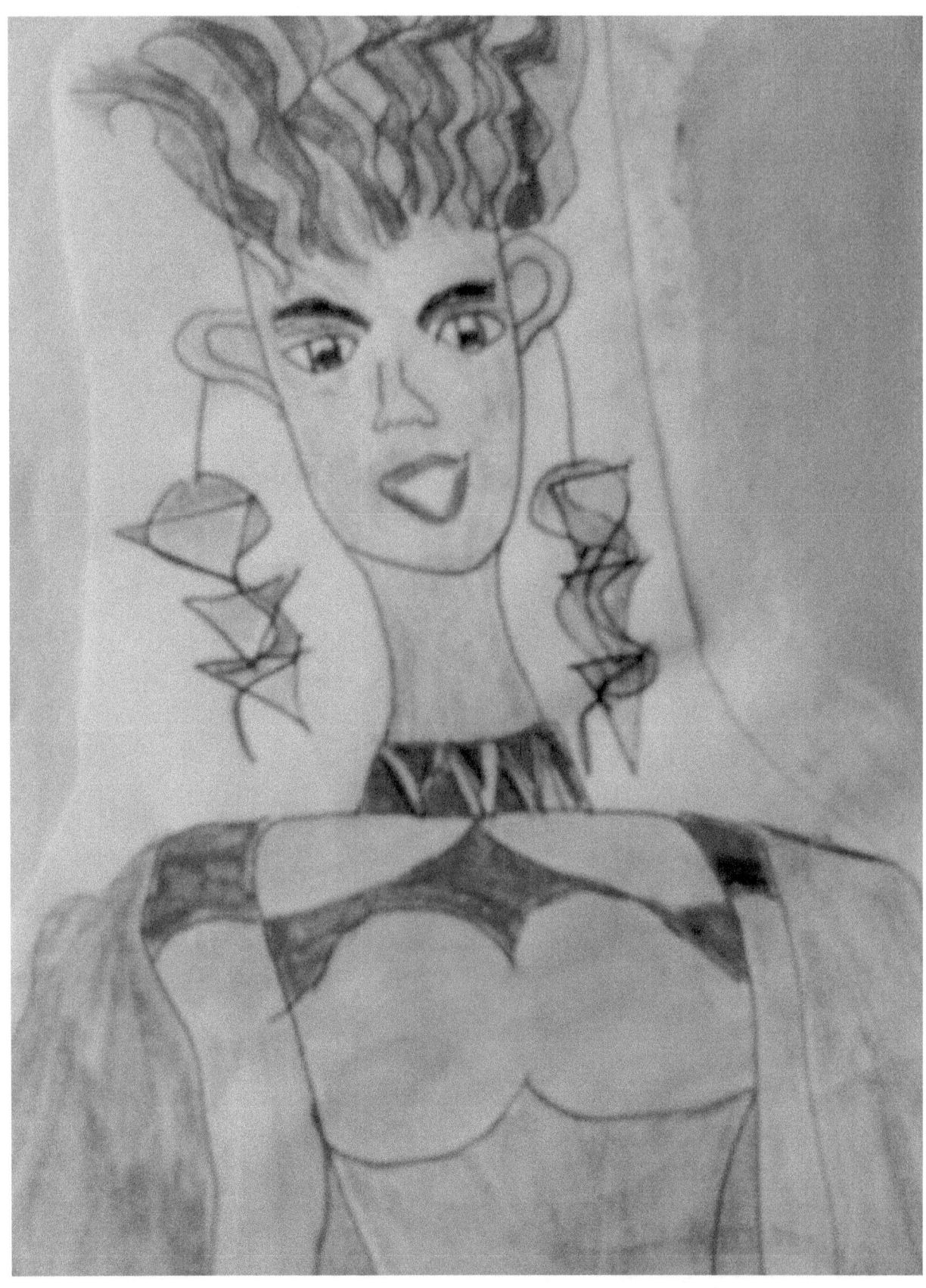

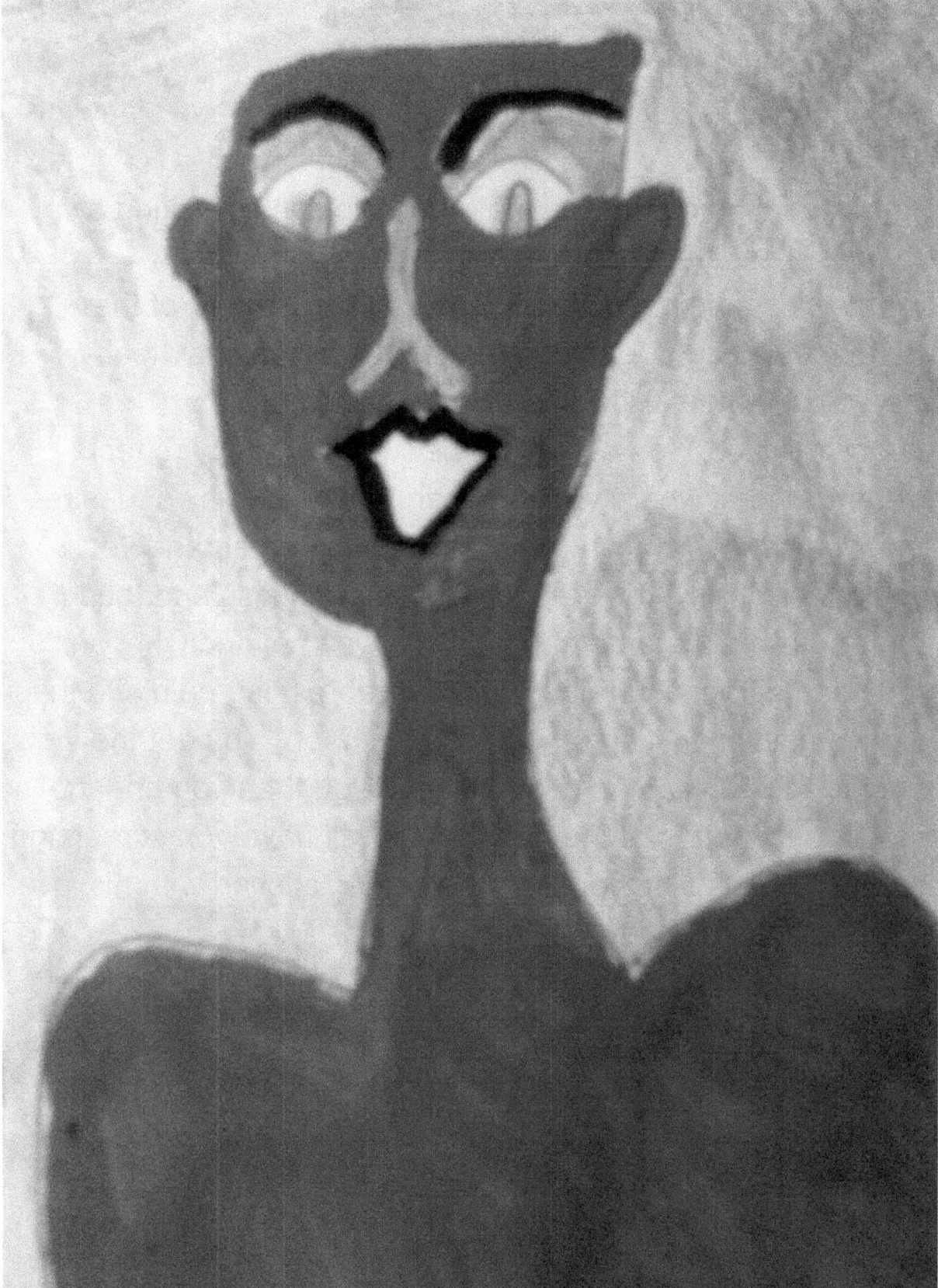

Chapter 3

Oh this loving is going I met the people of this man's day to day life. An

He has a lot going on but what I bring to it is not taking away from his pleasure. I bring kisses and my body to it

Fantasy ultimate destination to the heat and heart of the matters of loving. We don't get that in our busy day today lives. So we meet with in our minds with in

Our own space. You can call it view master the high tech dream world of where you go when you need a fix of desire and pleasure which can have you walking on air and you would think that you were there to love and kiss and touch. Oh this new tech game of passion is way beyond what sex and head games of the past with heartbreaking pain. Oh this way no pain or waiting on that other person. You get the view master and you see him and he sees you then you engage in a lot of encounters of the mind which will have you screaming in pleasure. Like chocolates you will be satisfied with his love and it will not change a thing in your life.

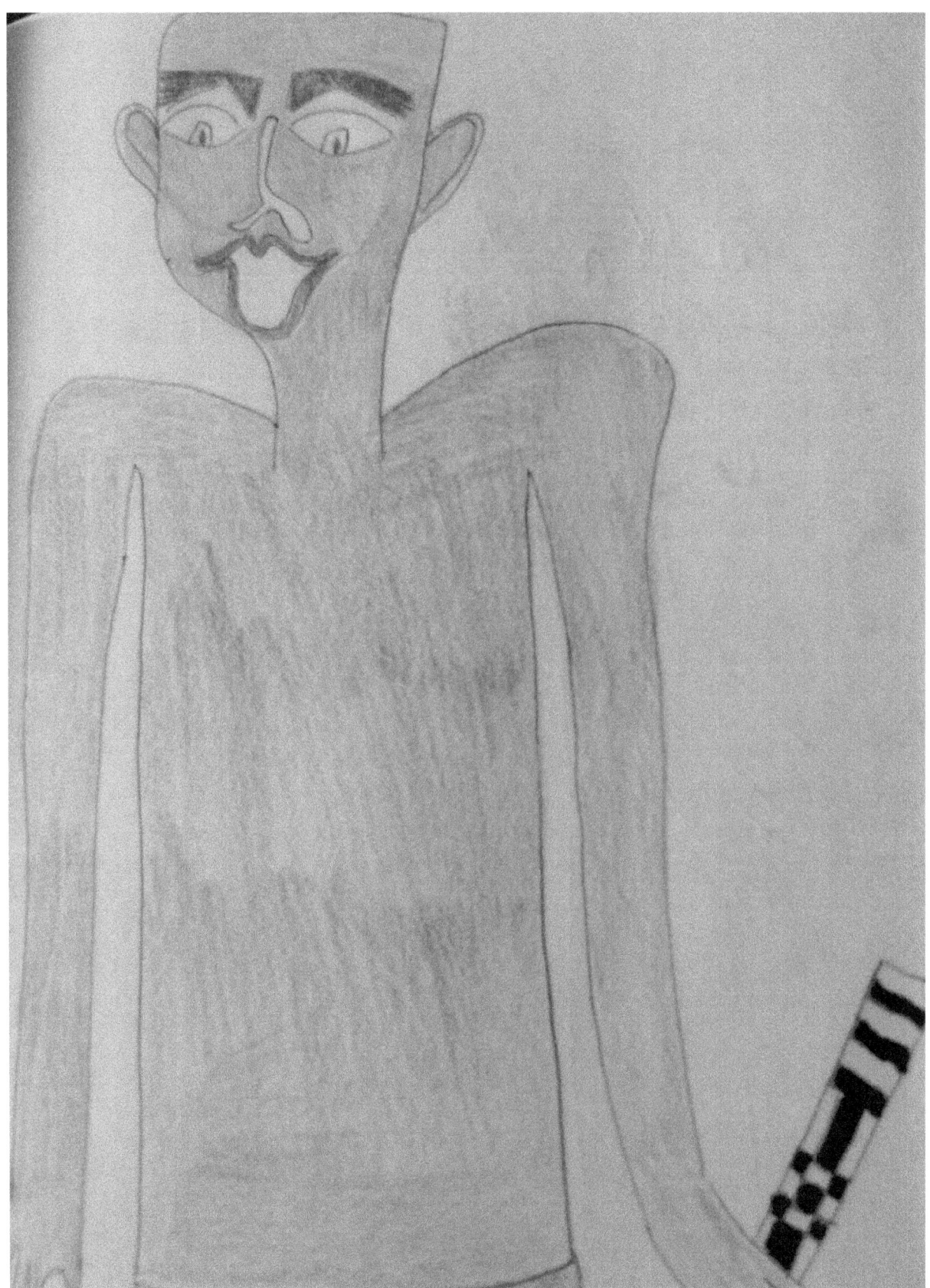

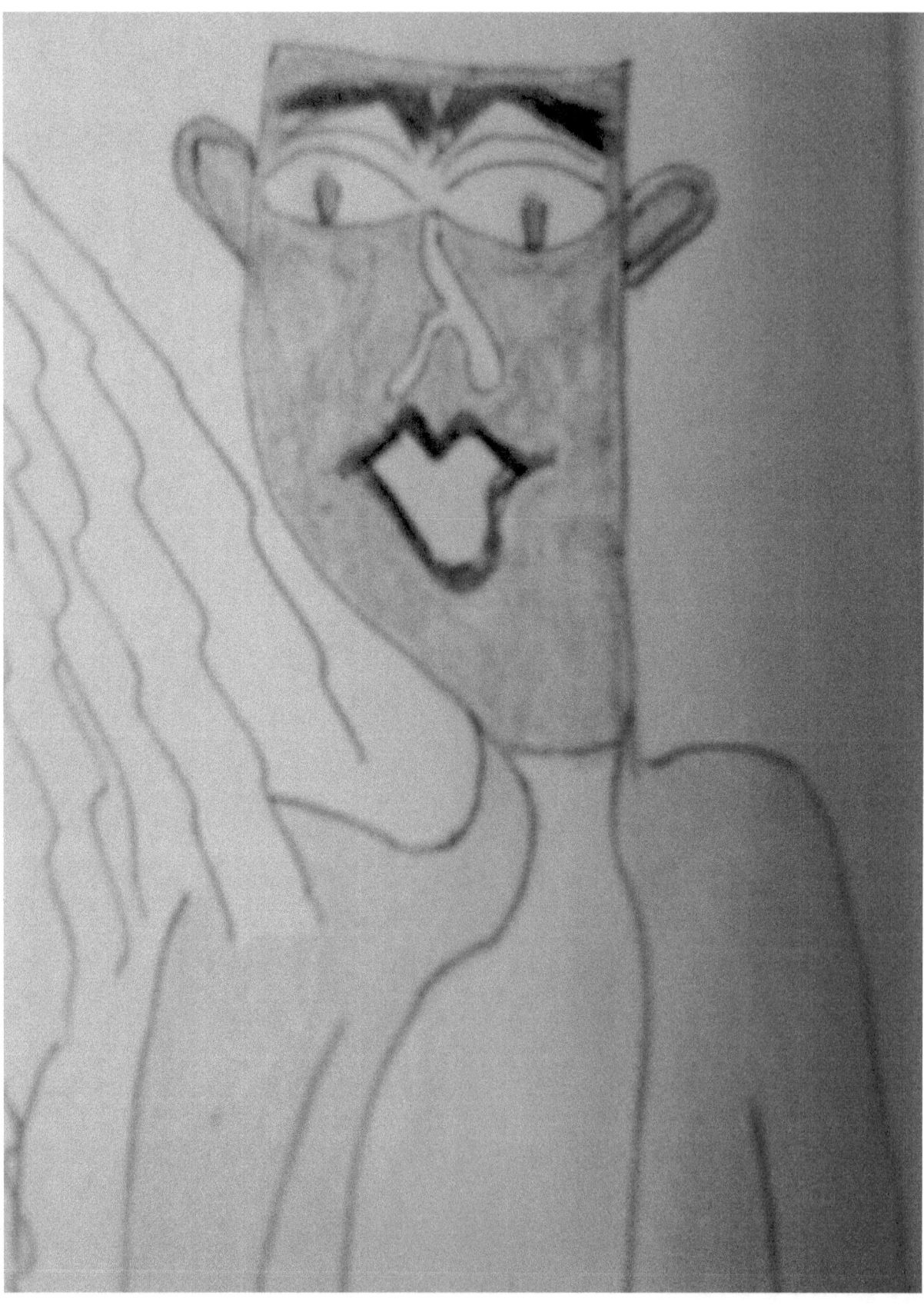

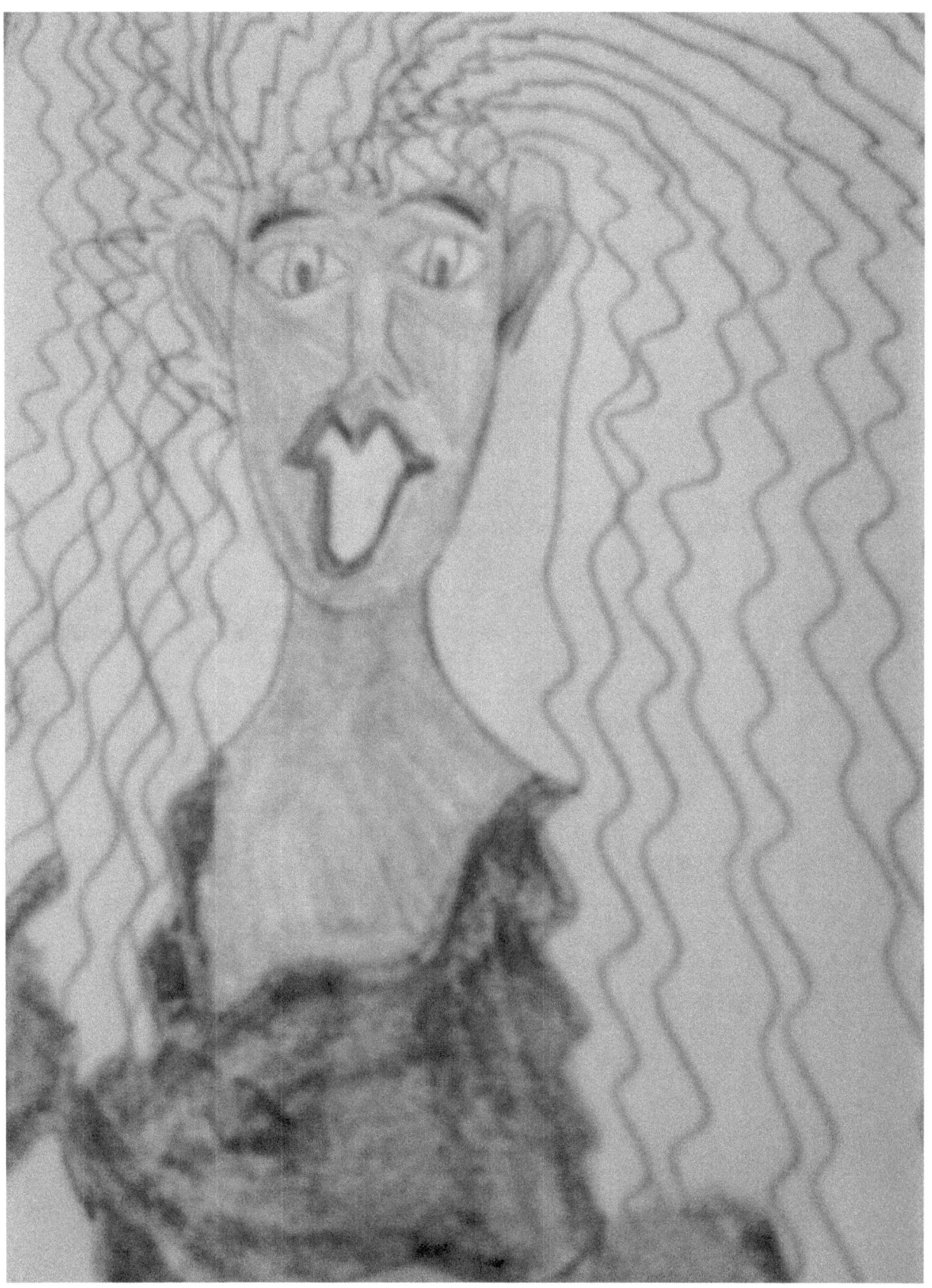

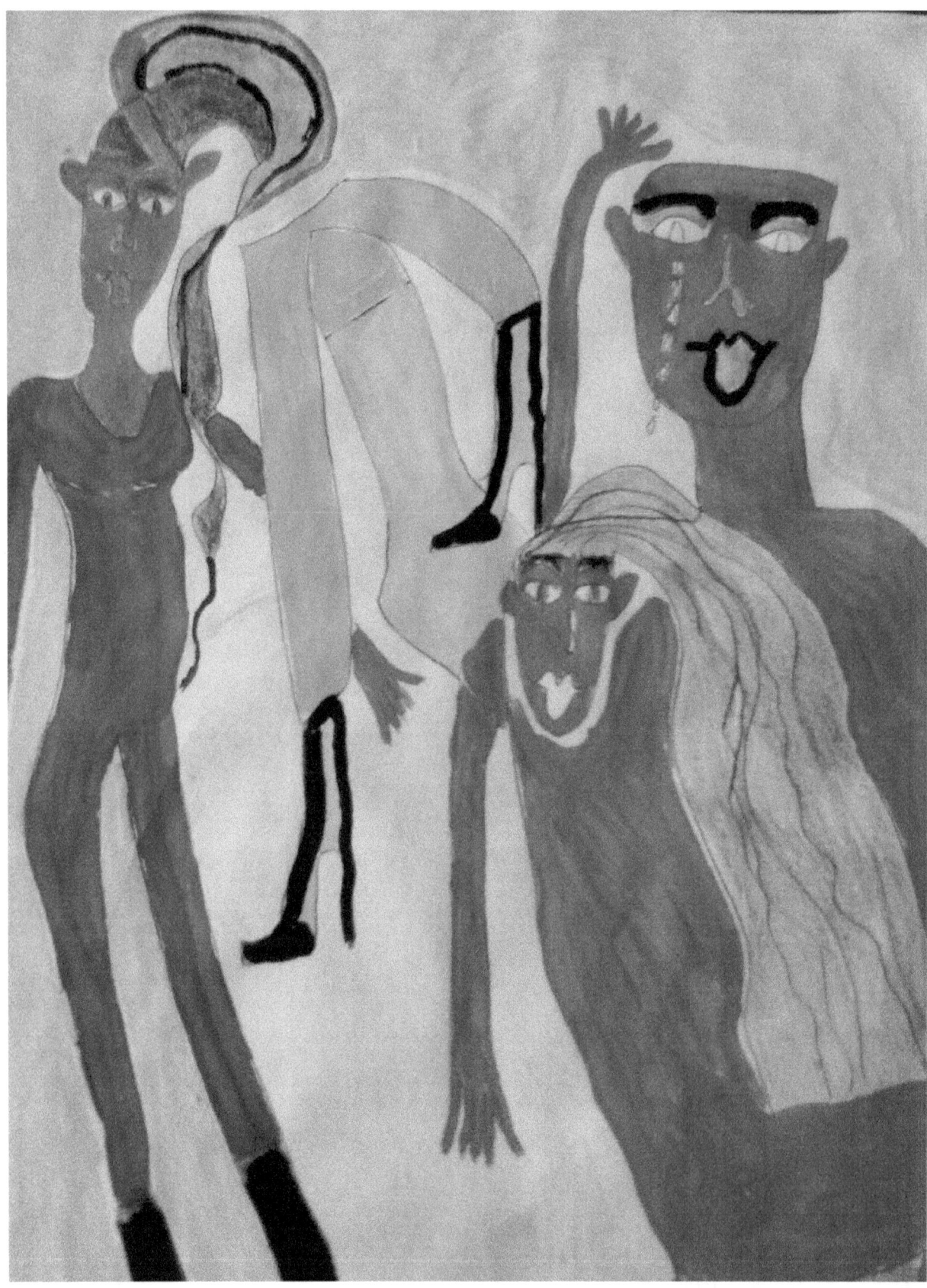

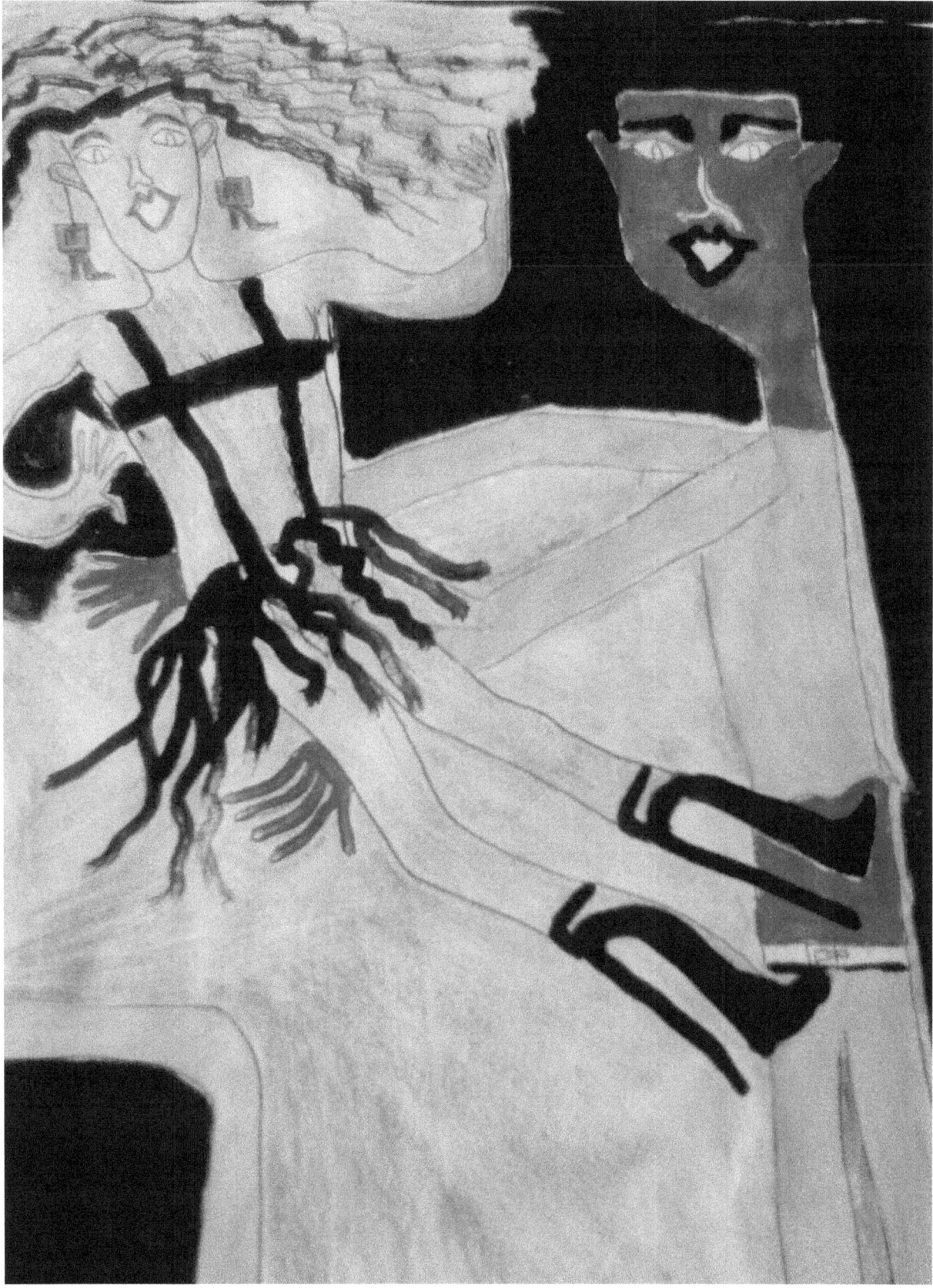

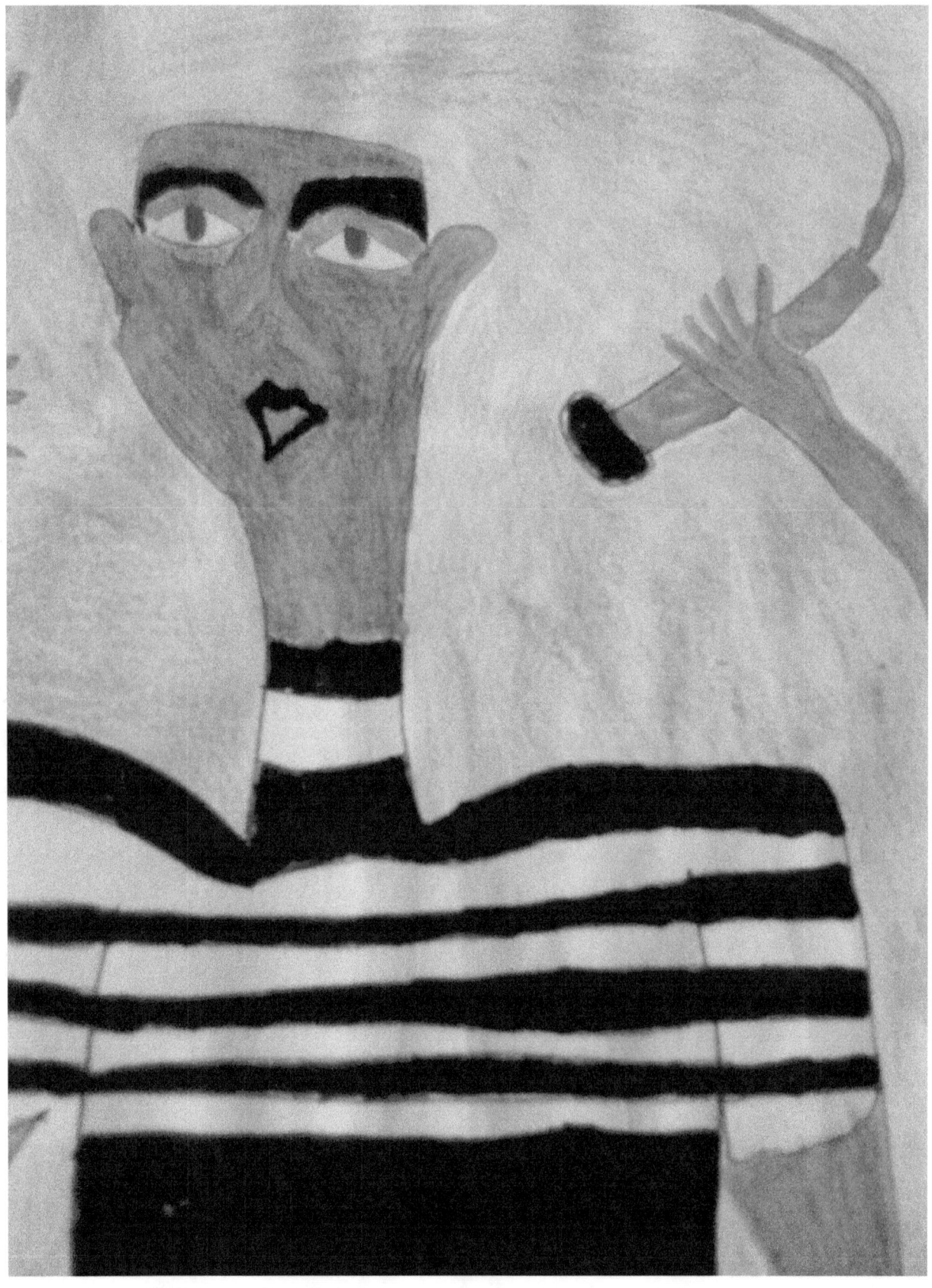

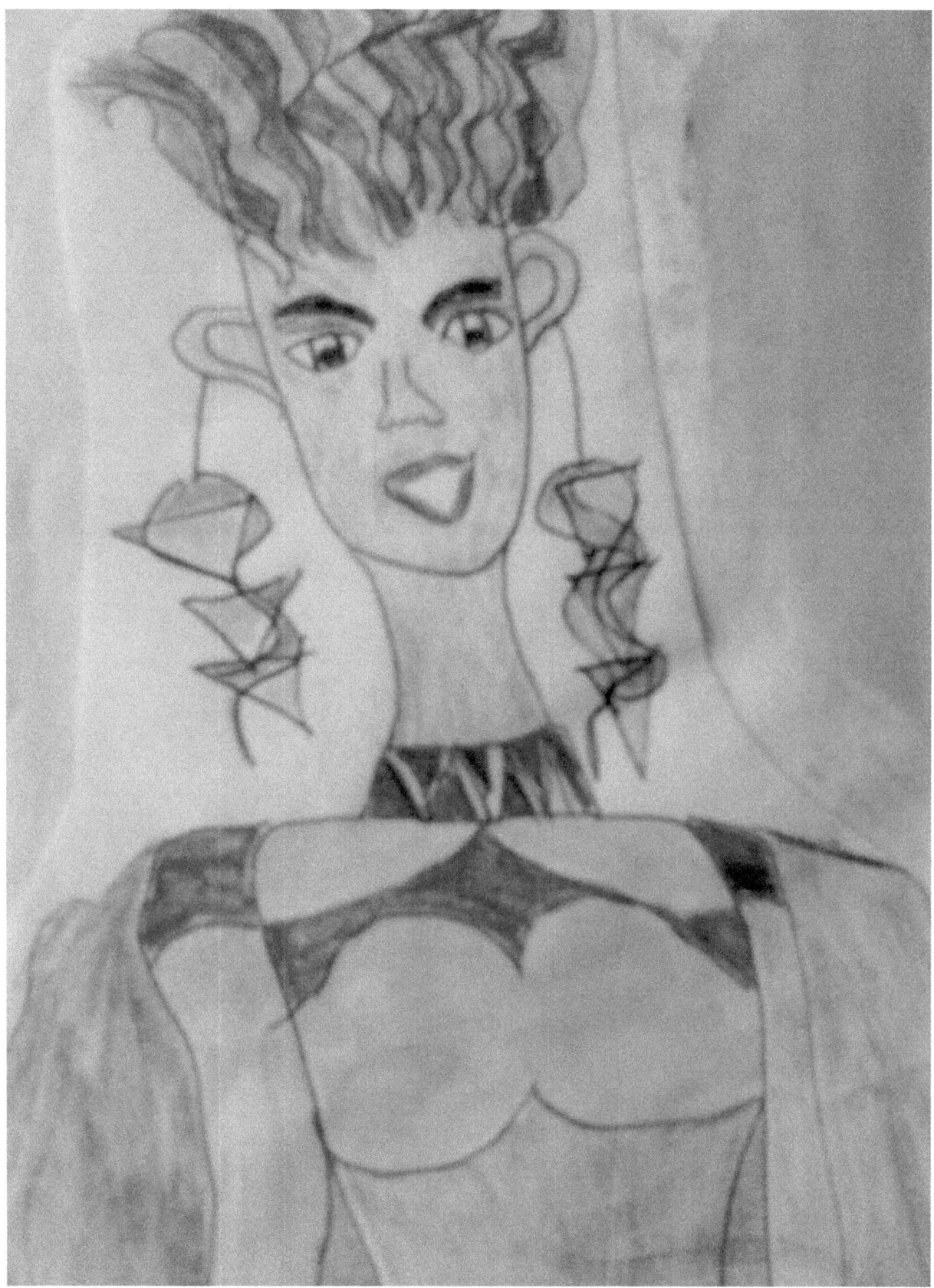

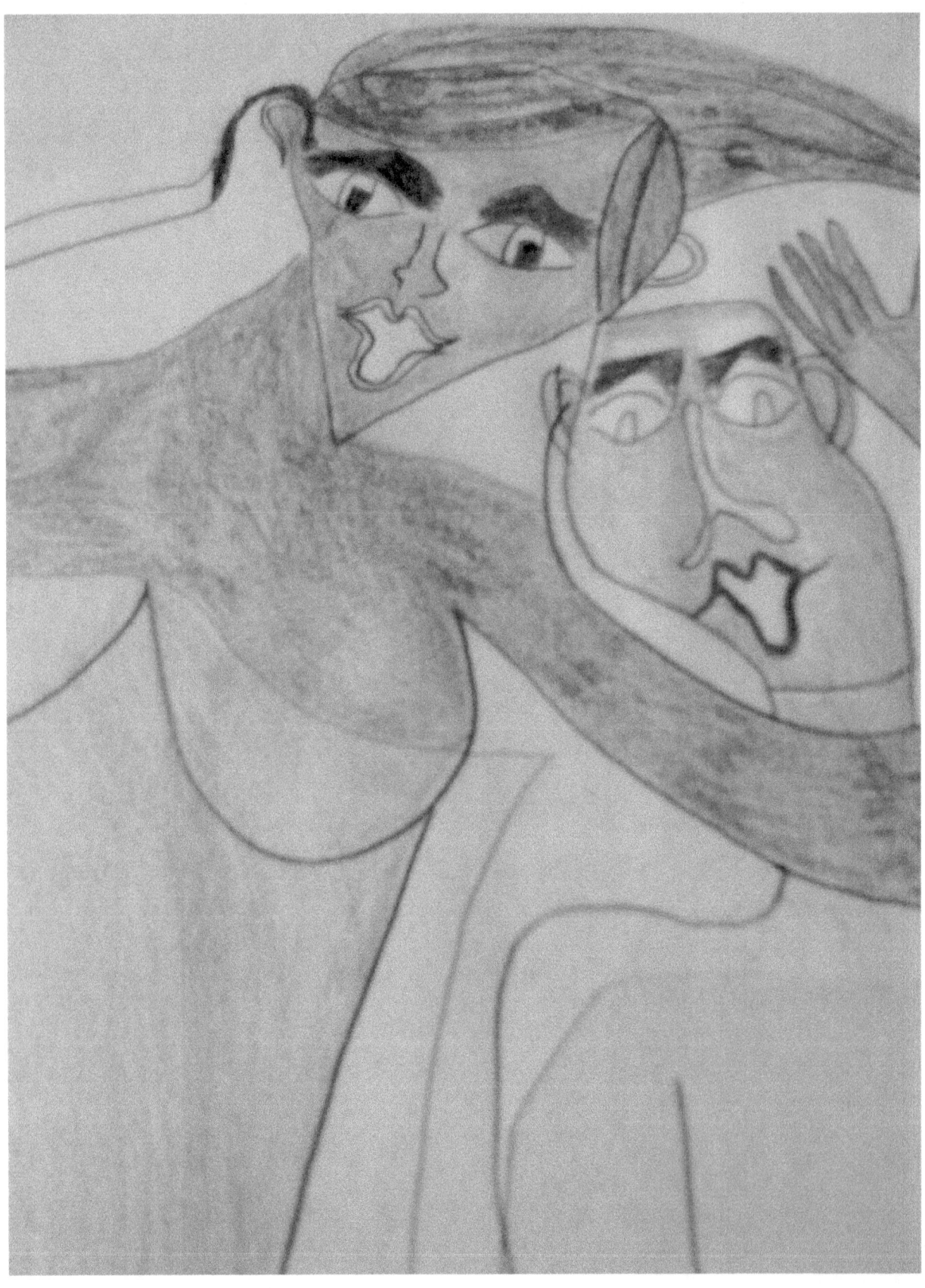

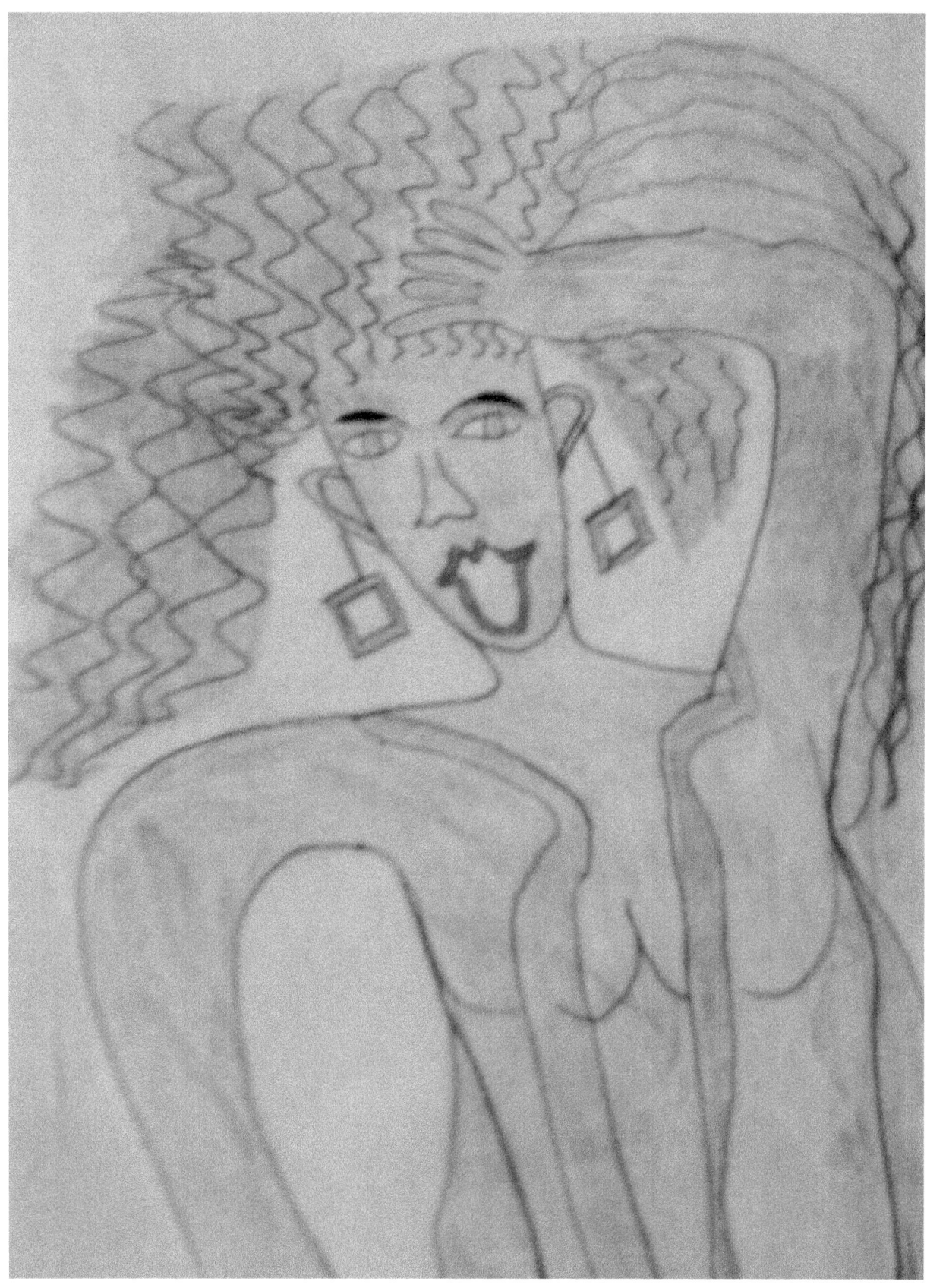

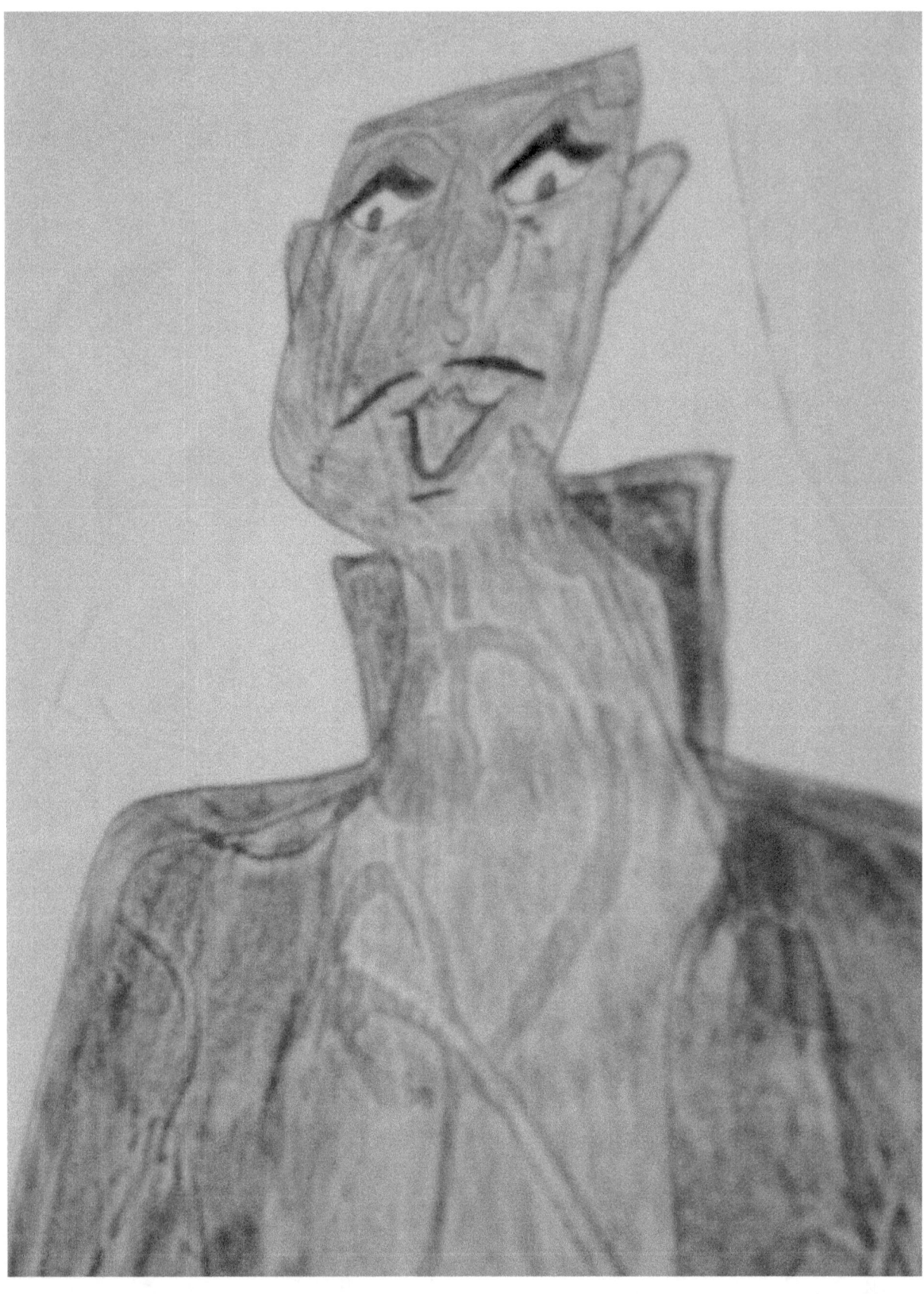

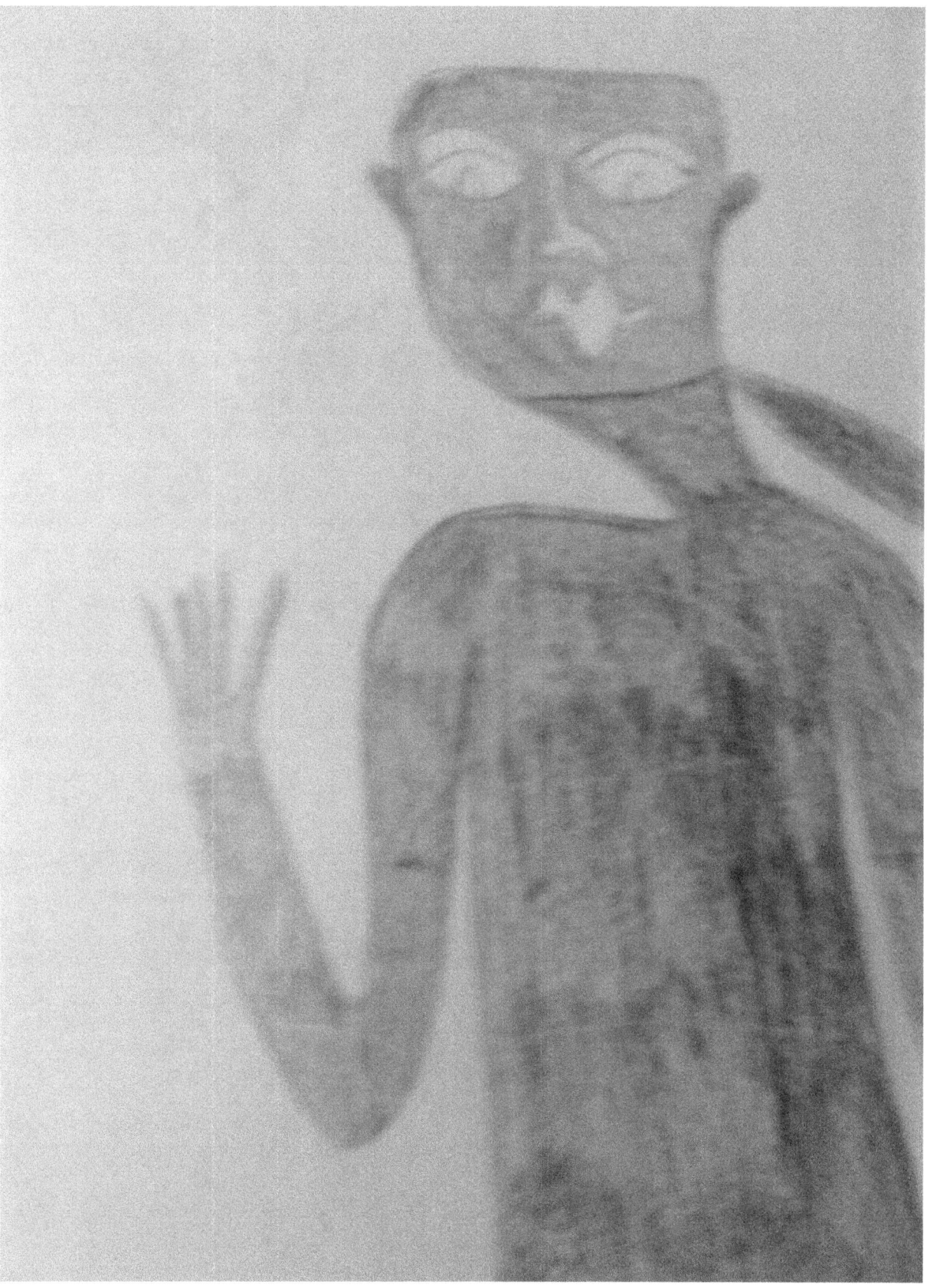

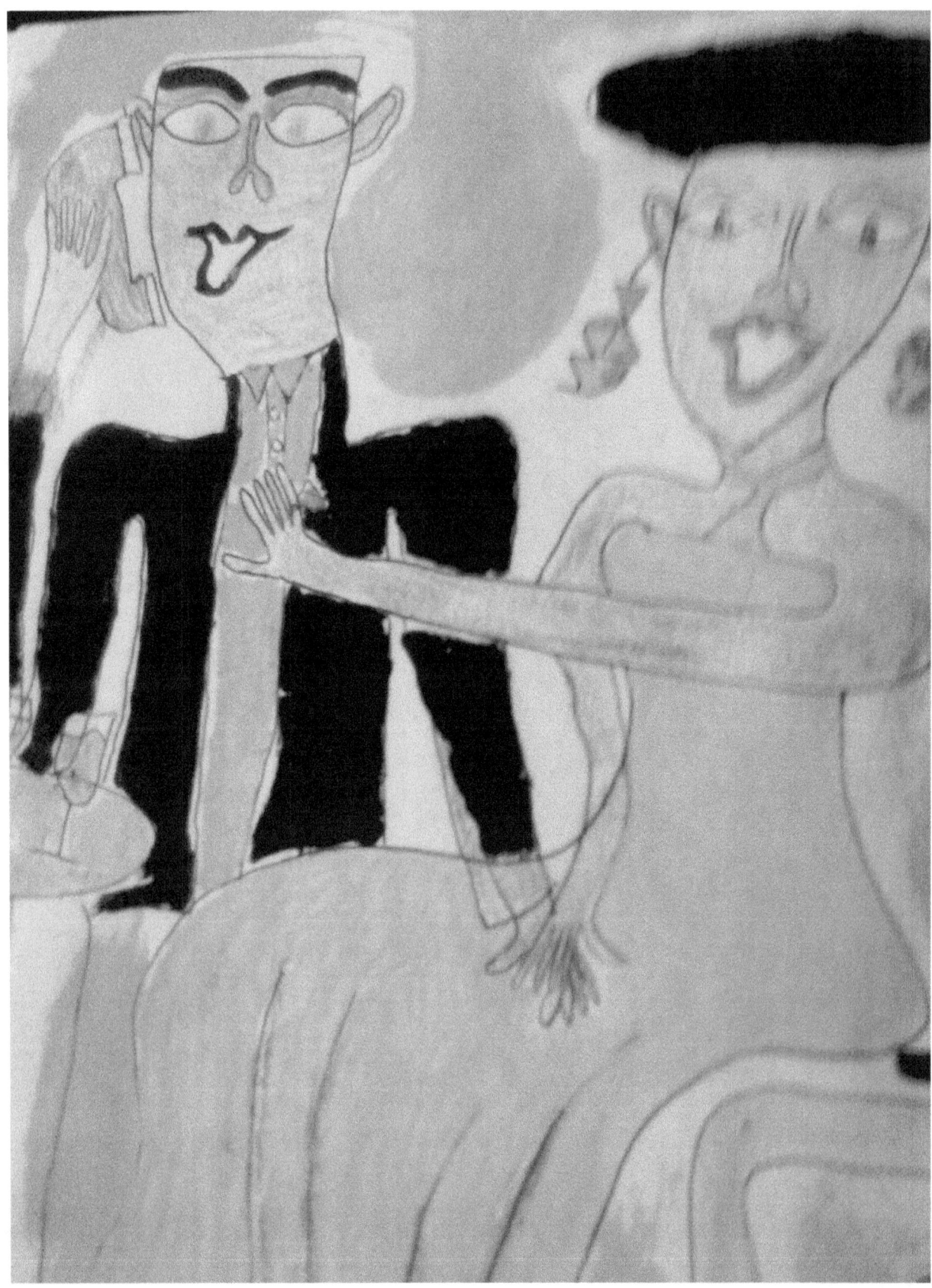

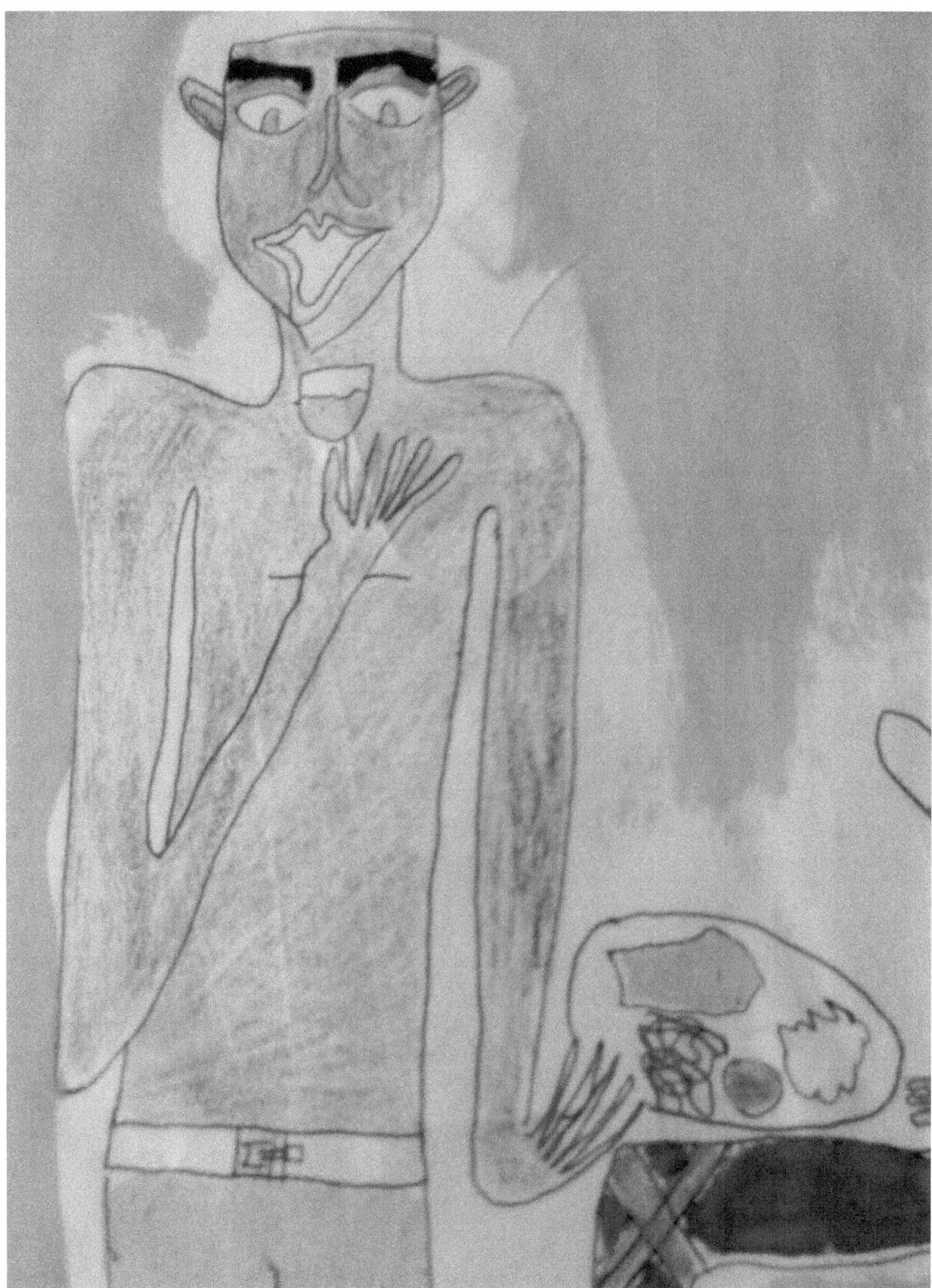

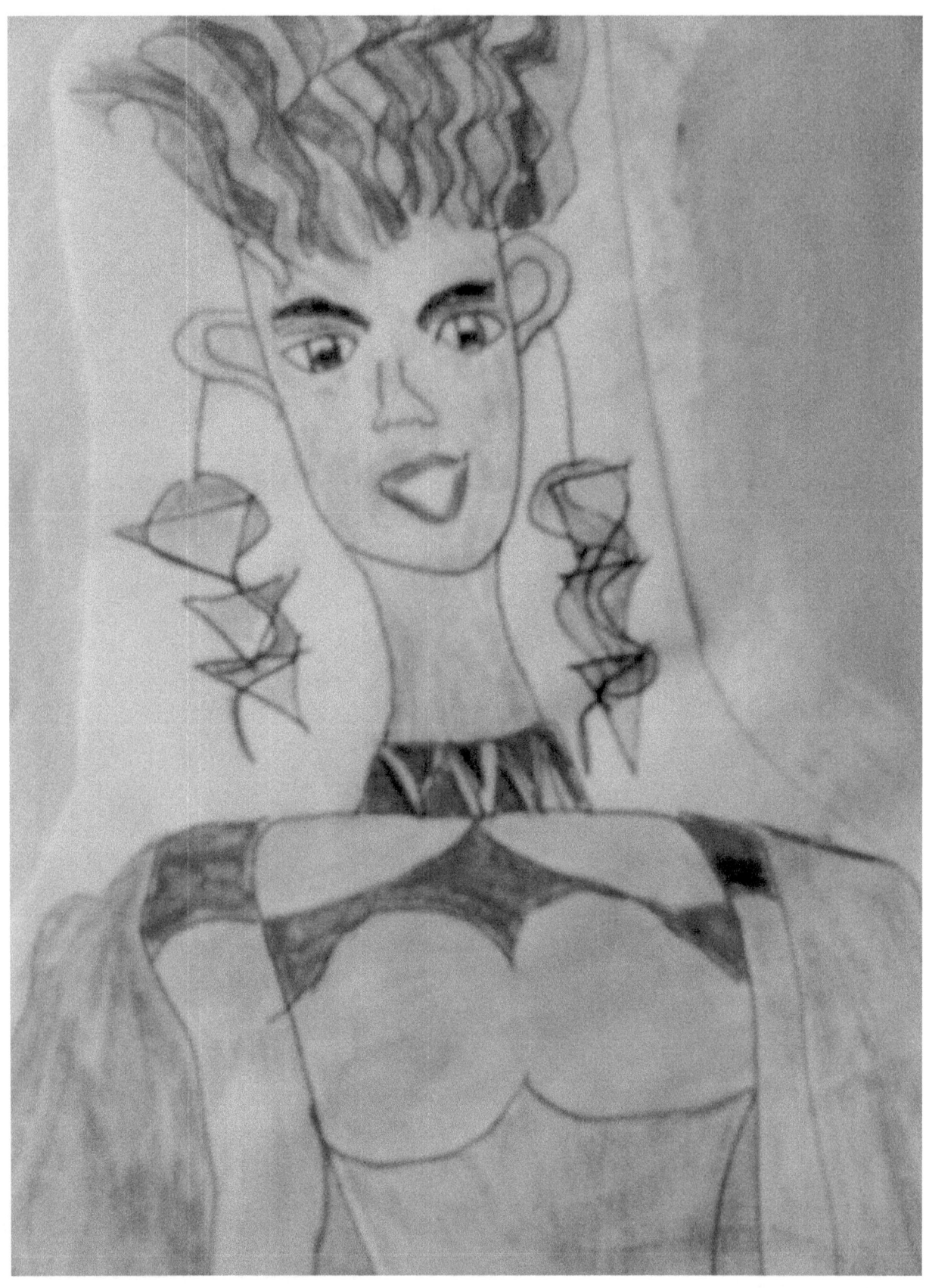

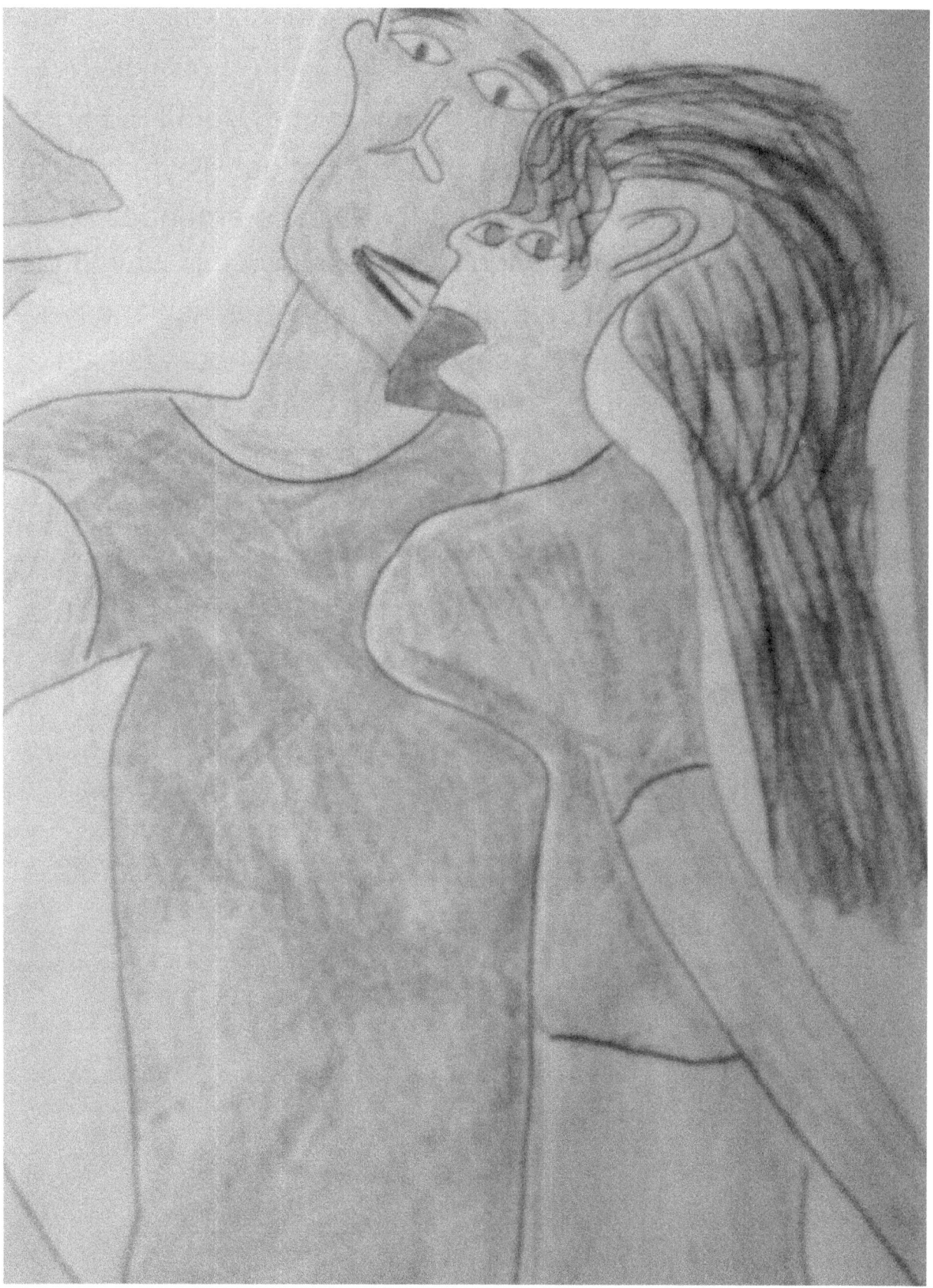

Chapter 4

So I feel so loved that I don't want to stop. And I get so into it I live for the view master and this hot guy Teyno which likes me to but I lose myself need to really be around him. Then I want the sex and loving fastasy always this way to the point where I am out of control. I don't want the view master toy any more I go to his house and we spend hours talking and fucking until

We set it right by acting out the very fastasys which got us to this point in the first place.

He takes my hand and before we make out.

He says some of his poetry to me to get me to that place where he wants me.

Hugging Drone

You got me in your eye
But you all fly, sexy in the sky
You move over my world
Steaming my view of what I need so much of you
You drop the note at my
Door step
I look and say
Baby what's this
Oh its a note for your lips
To repeat and say
As I feel your passion
From the words you speaking back to me

Sexy!

Turn This On Yeah
Say you like the flow
And how I go with your
Loving
Oh don't you think I know
Or got those same feelings to
Oh I want you
And no other will be able
To do in this
Between me and my desire for you.

Looks Hot
You got fire and sexyness
Loving is your gift
You are that kiss on
This part of my body baby
Always to get me alone
So you can
Cool me from that hate
In this world
Oh I be looking for you.

Chapter 5

So we pore this wine and other mixed drinks to the heart of
this love.
Now we drunk at the thought of so much of
These feelings letting loose the Blum of our
Roses and lips into
Kisses and touches
Of what's going down
Between you and me
And its more then being
Drunken you know!
 I walk with the knowledge of knowing that I am in your
passion
Oh to the clouds I say with this as my lips love
And kiss your style.
Keeping it going is not
Even an issue of so much going on within this.

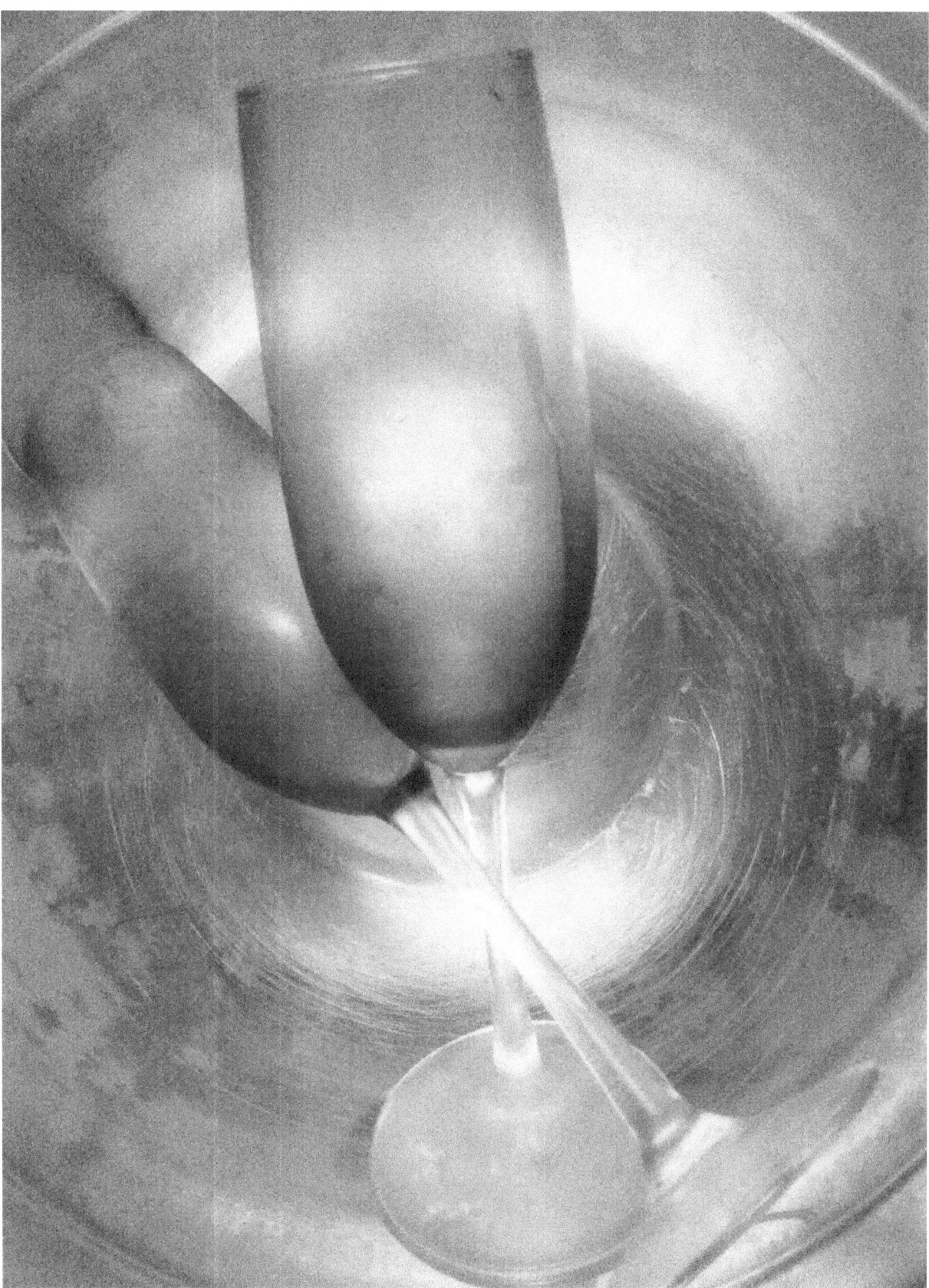

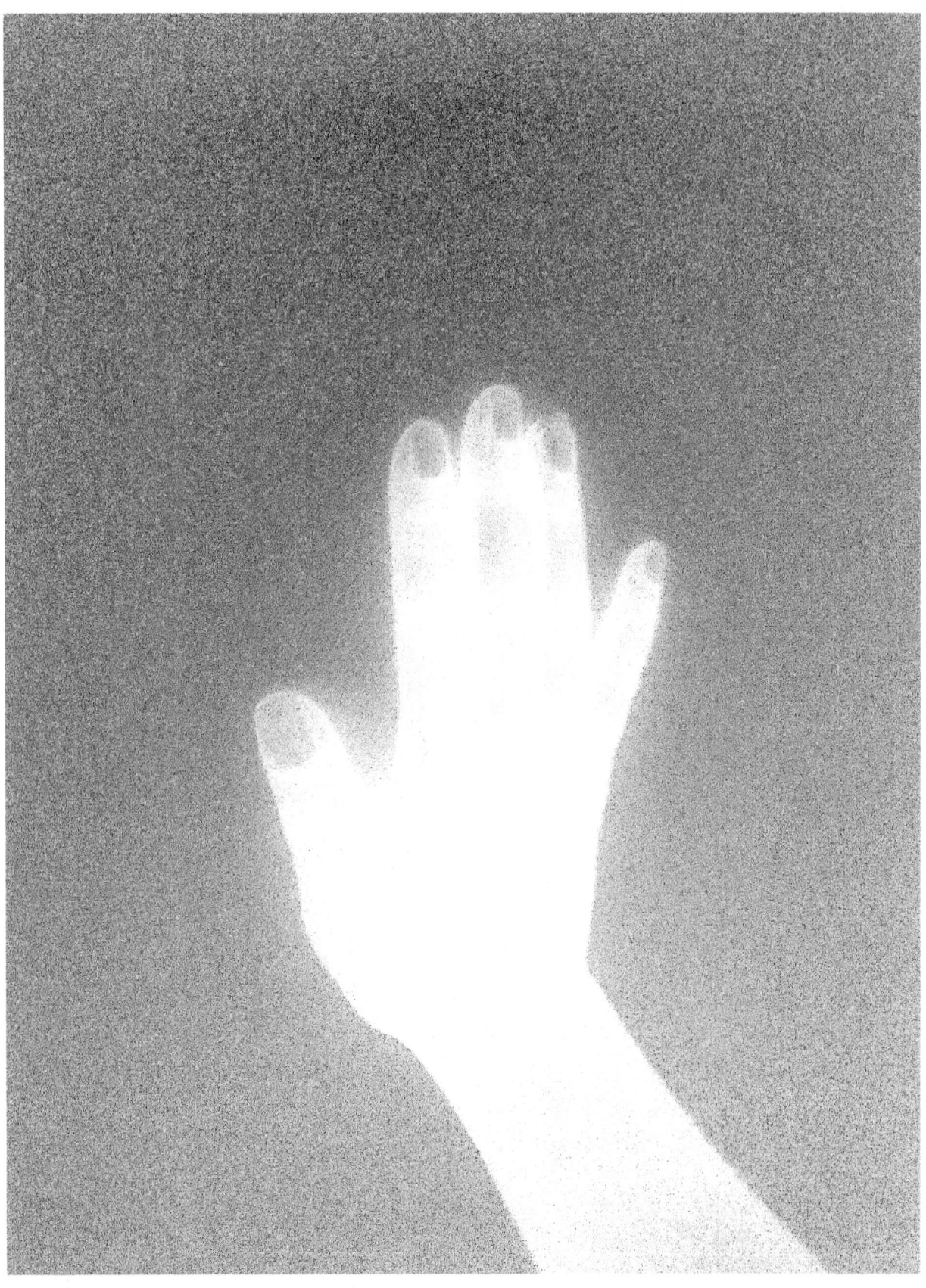

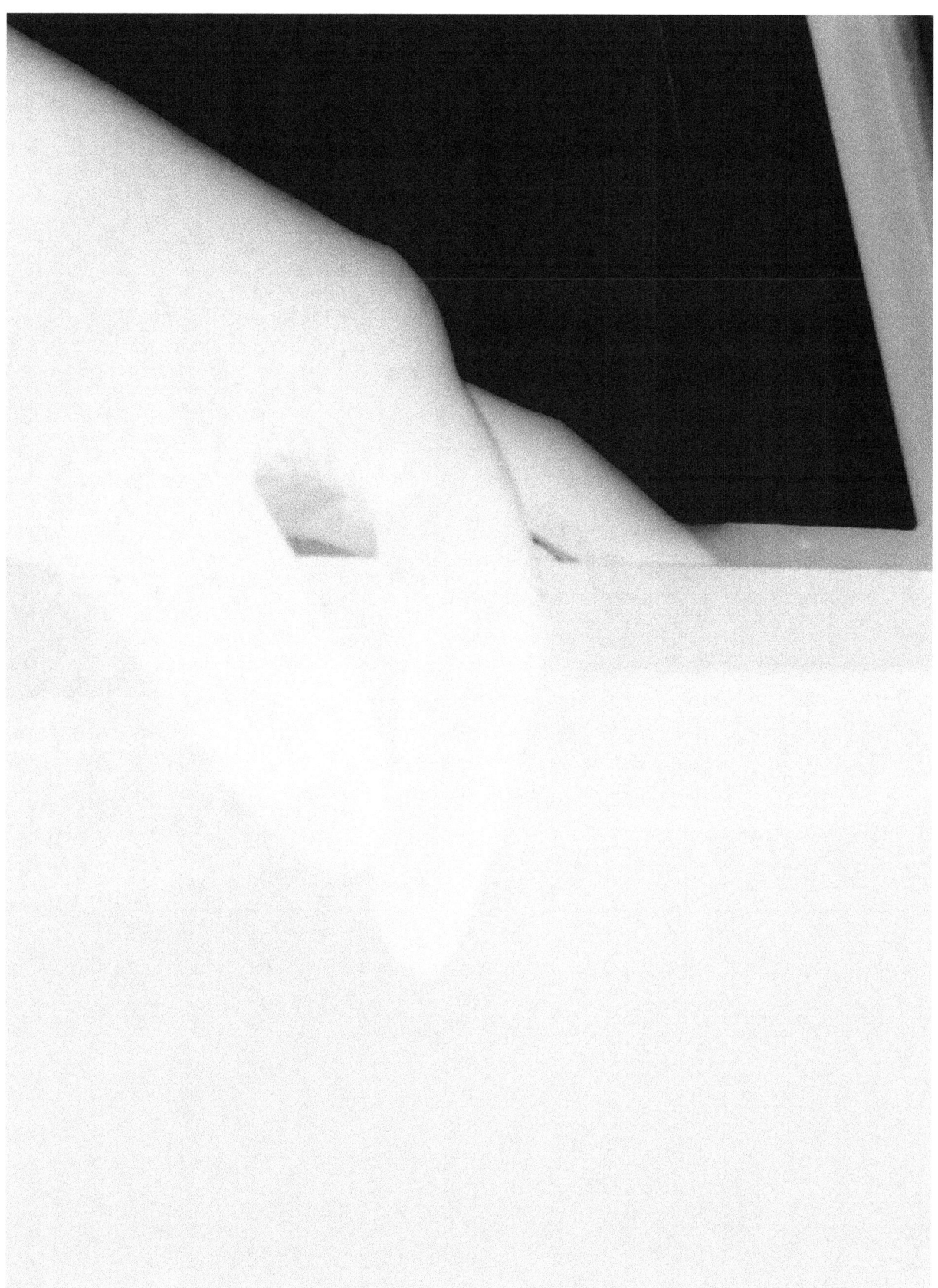

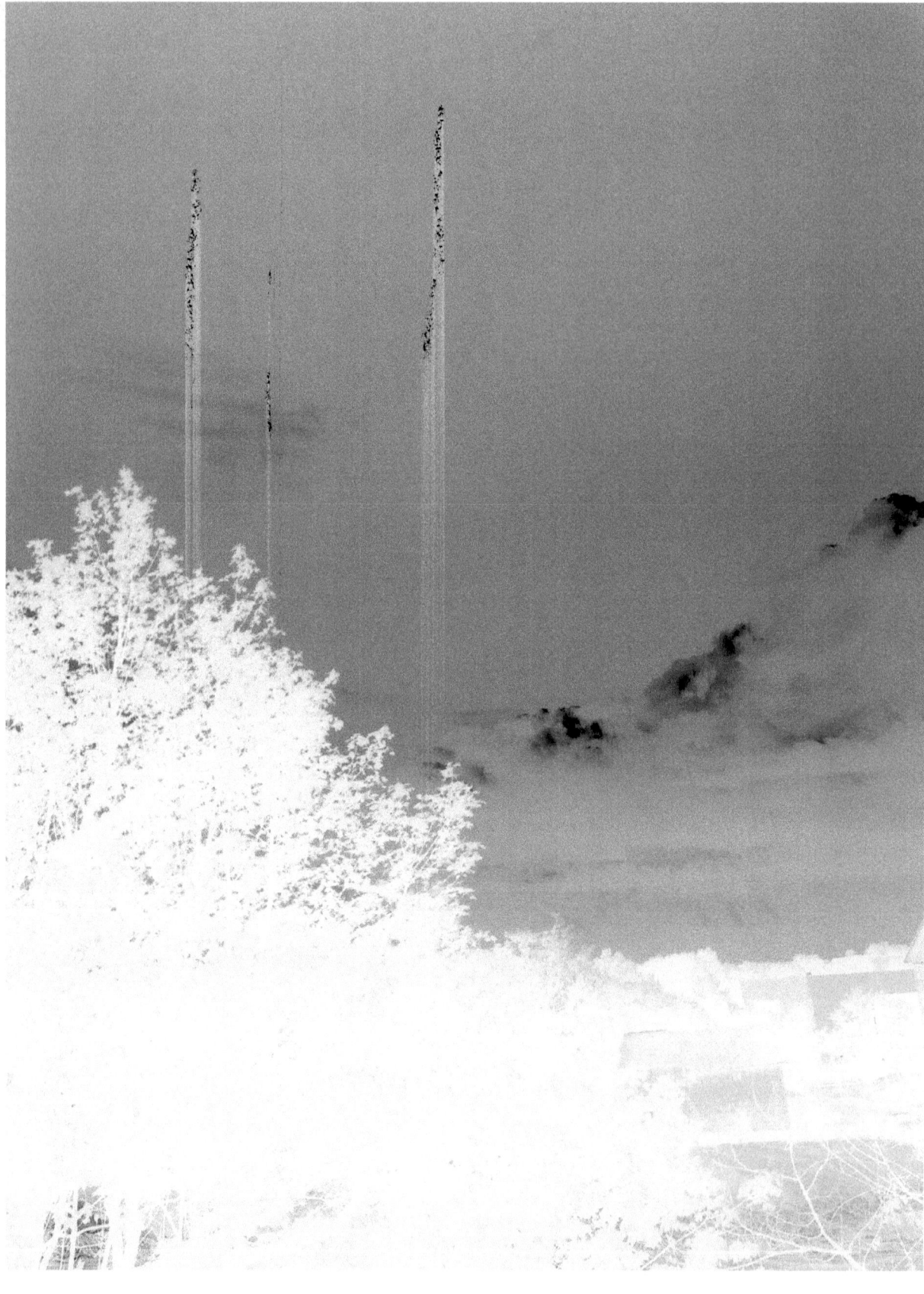

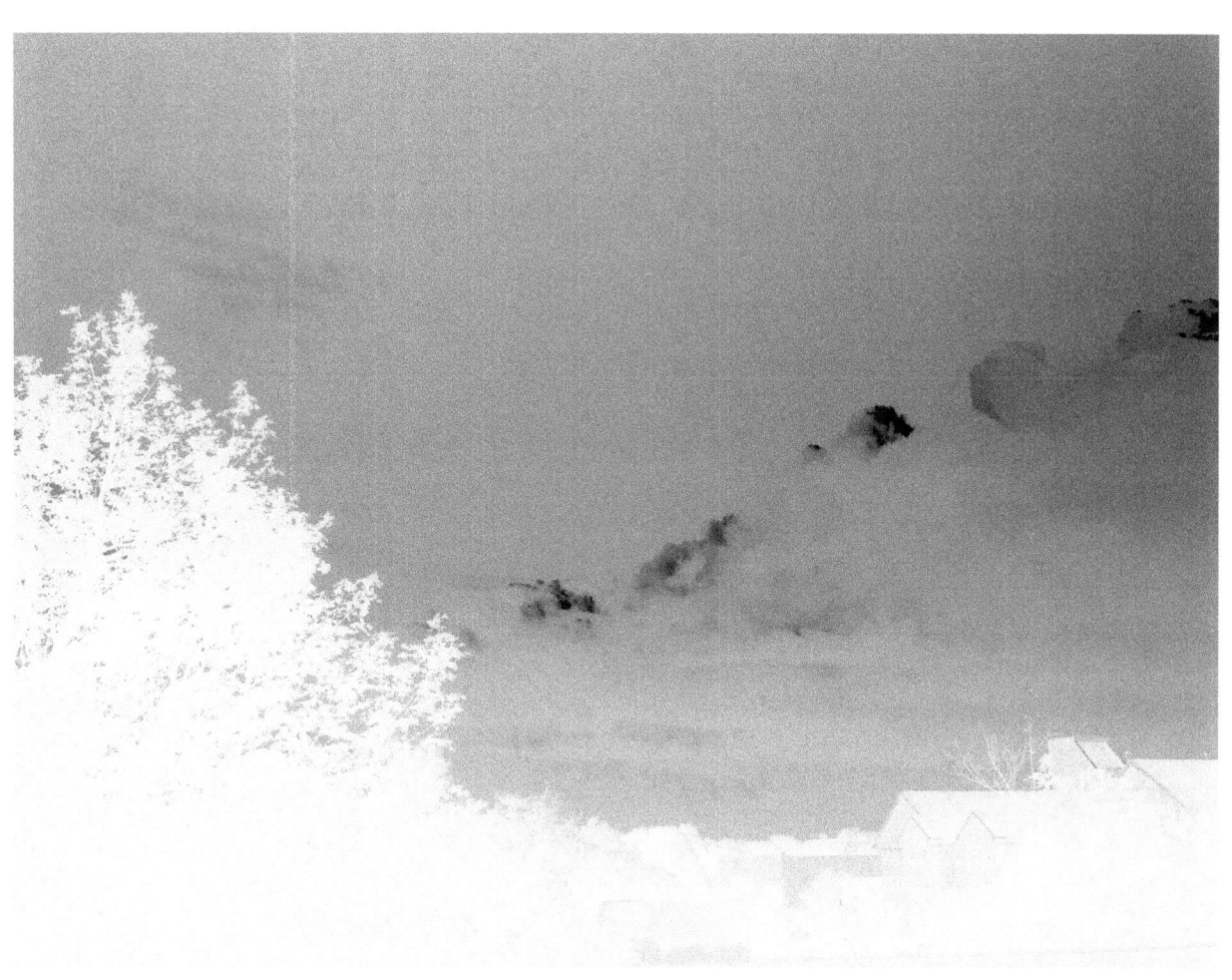

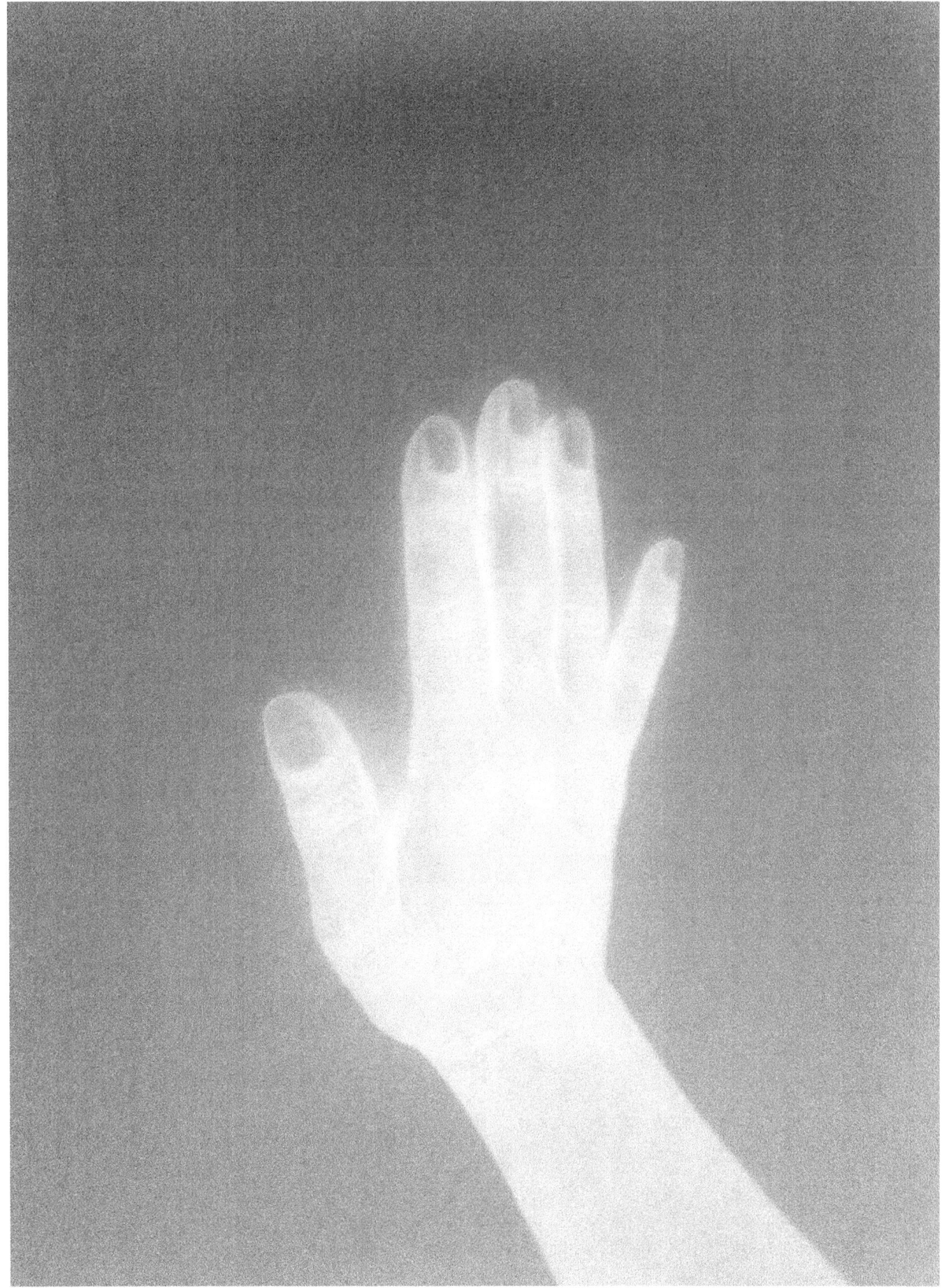

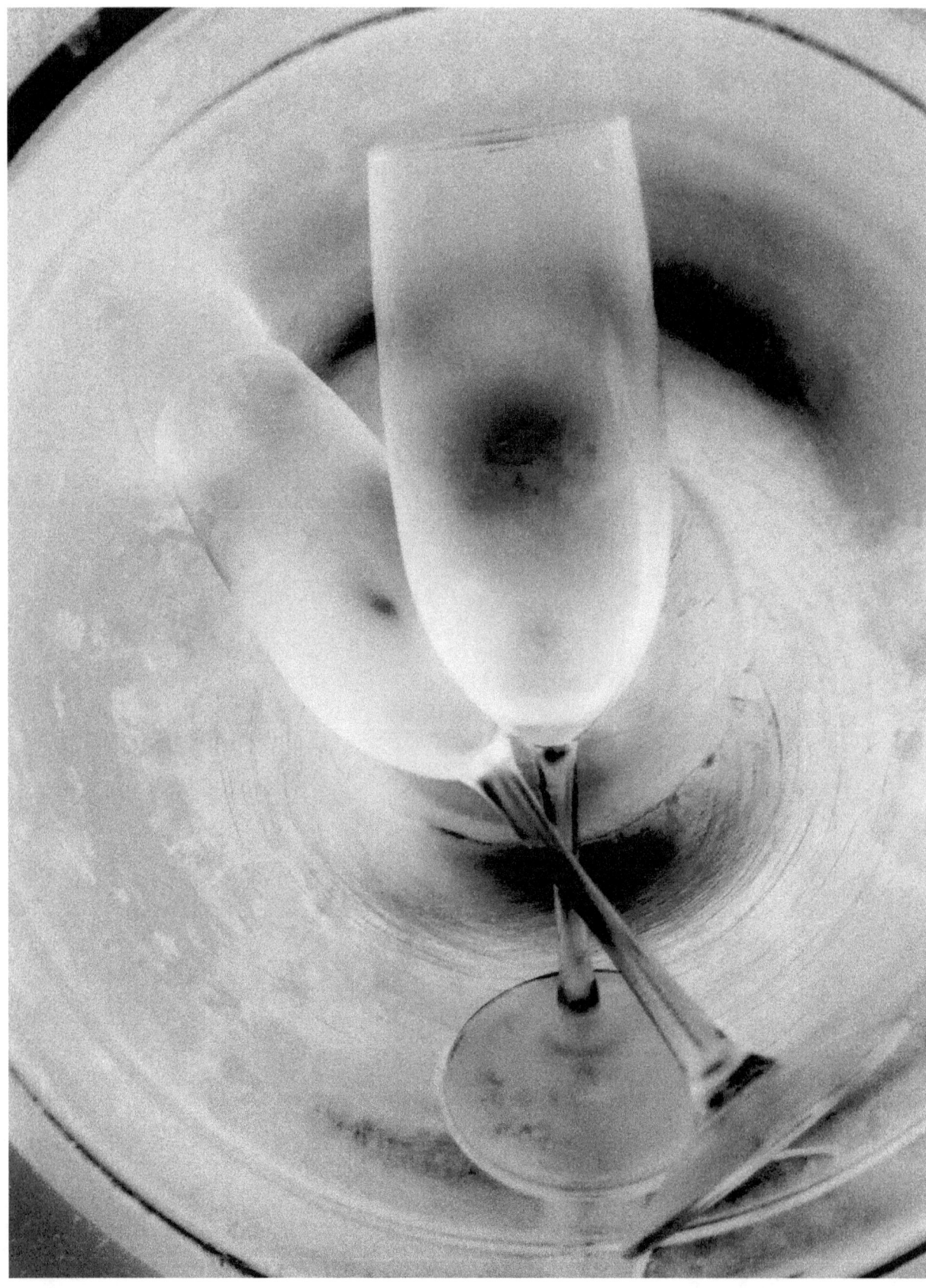

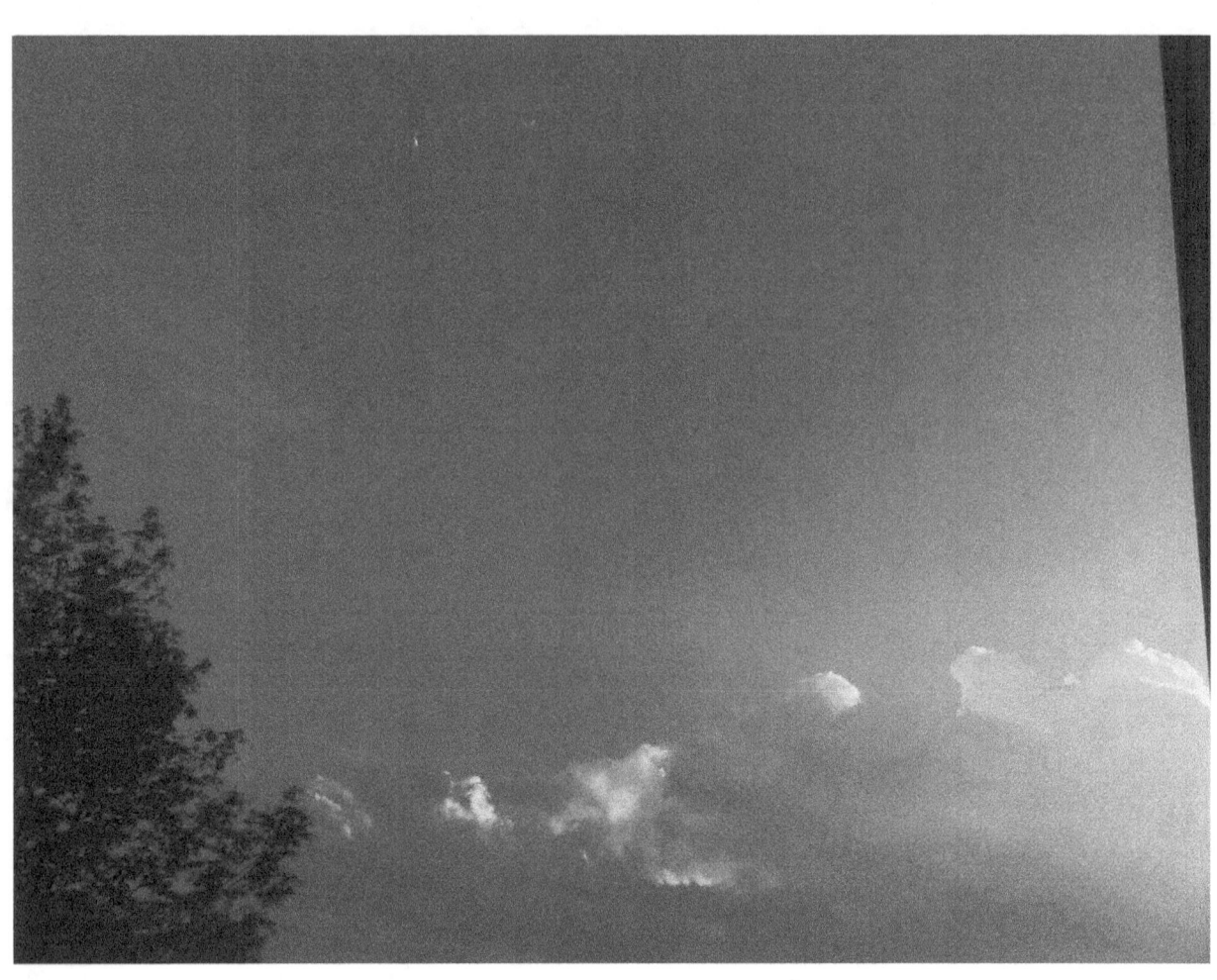

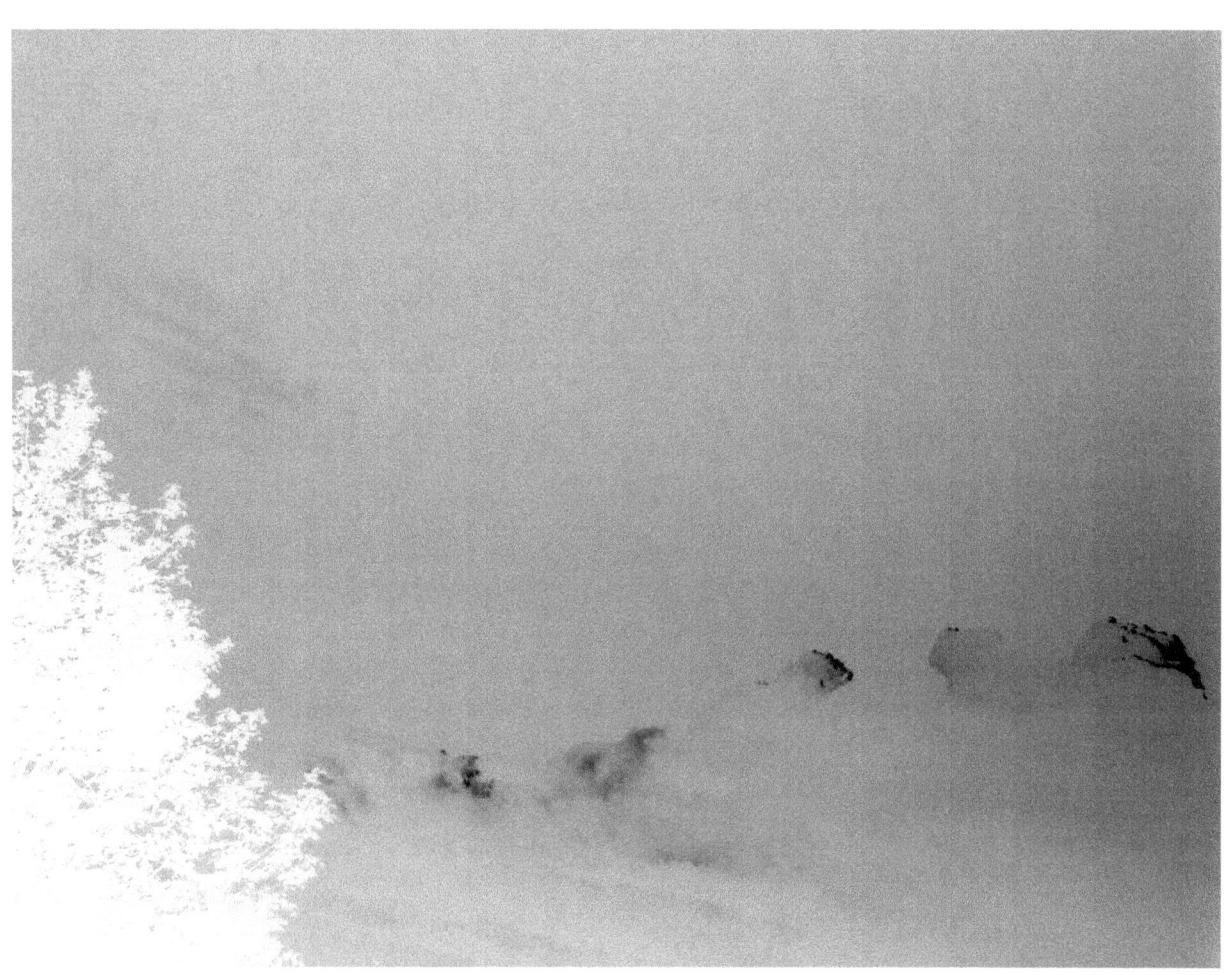

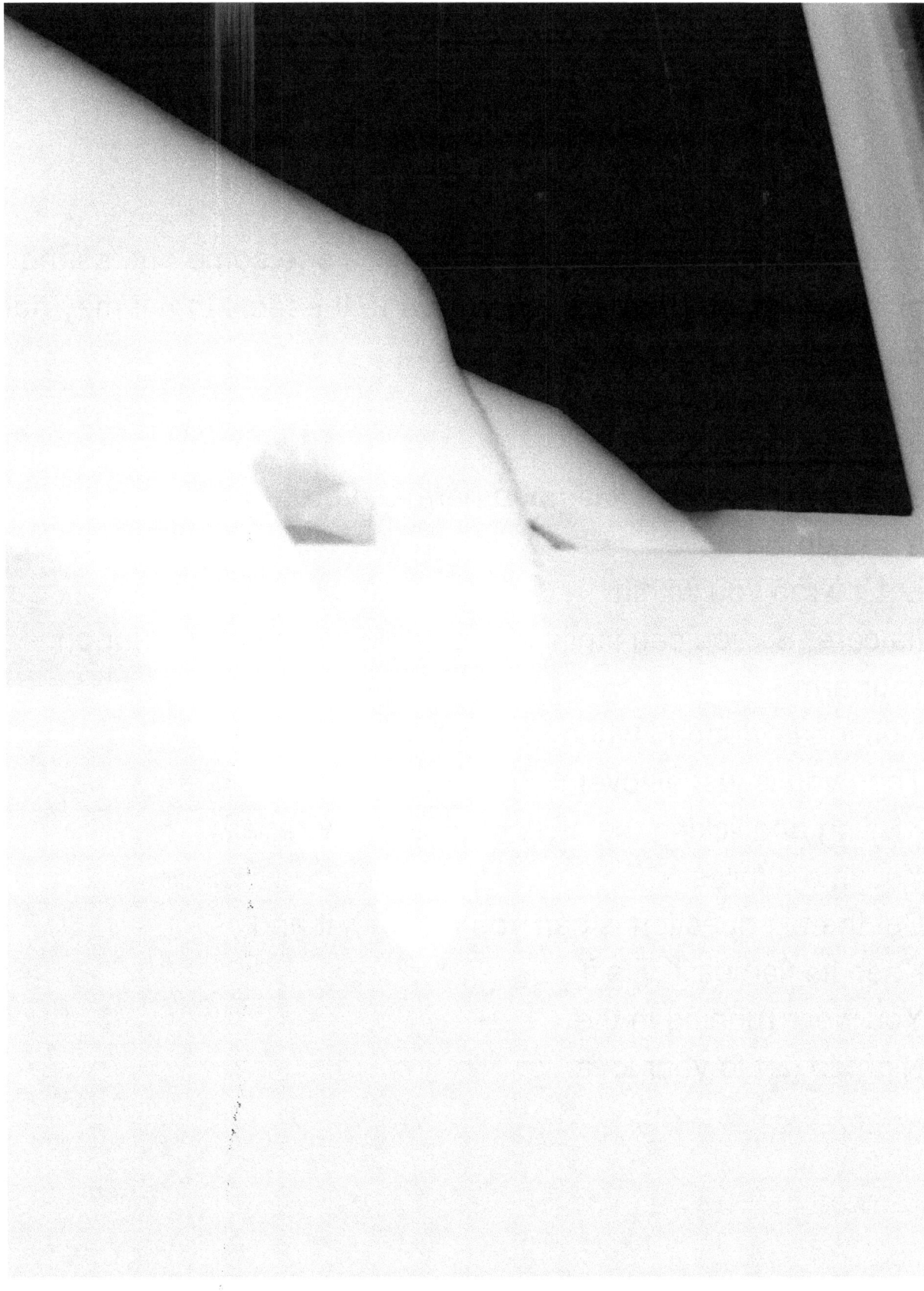

Chapter 6

You Got Me In Thee Air

  Oh love I funny this way. It makes you see some one as the only one for you. It makes you blind to the facts that it may not be who

You were to be with for

Along time.

But I do know this if it is not a harm to you

If you do find love

Let it wrap you within

Its care. So you can smile at the world with your warrior on your arm.

Nothing is stopped when its like this yes

Then you is just all over it

Kissing and licking the style of all which wraps

You into it miles.

But the big question is can you run with it and

Keep its flames lit like if

You were running in the

Night to get to your love.

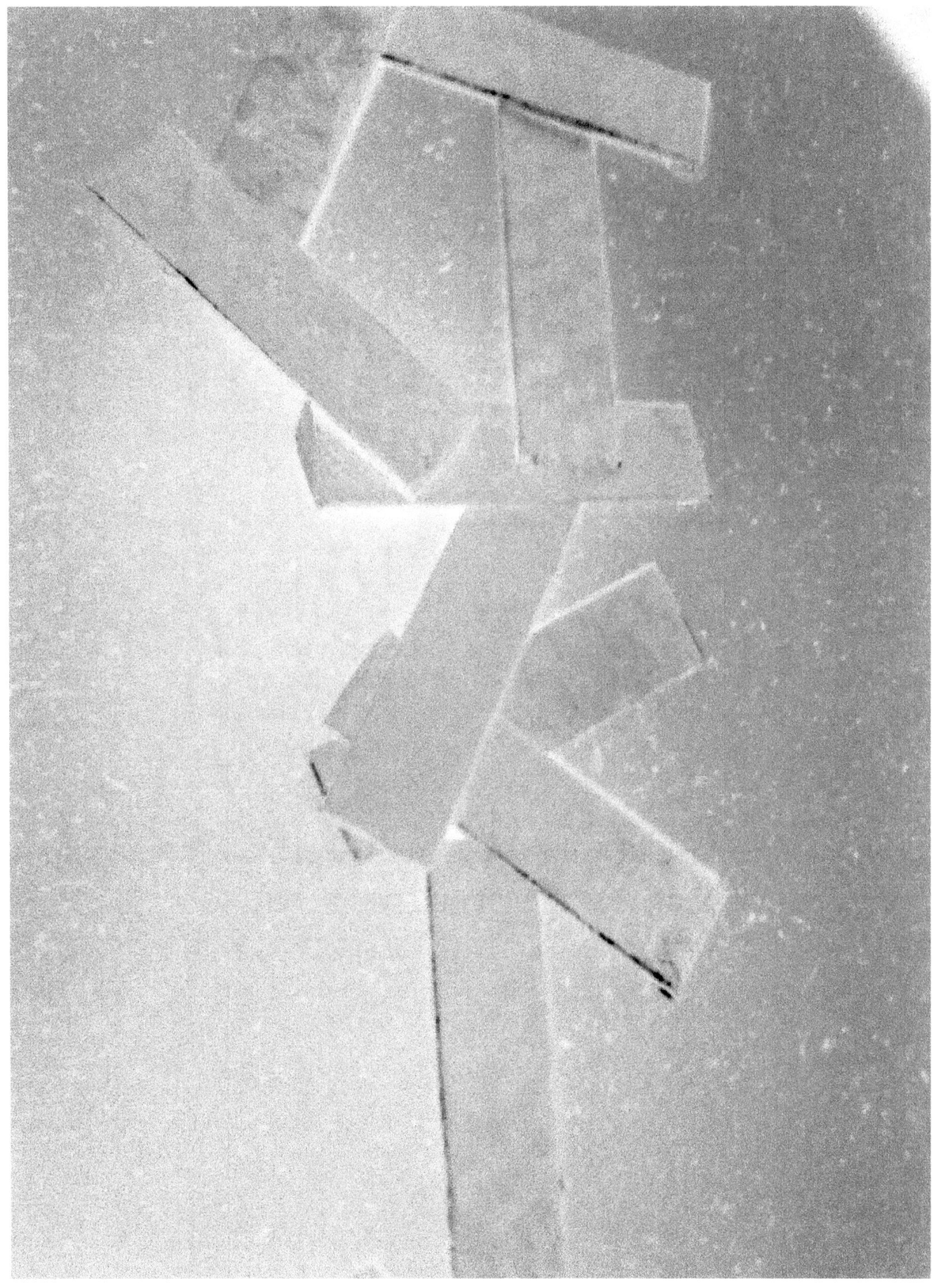

Gum is what gets you to
Fresh kissing all over
What you and him love.

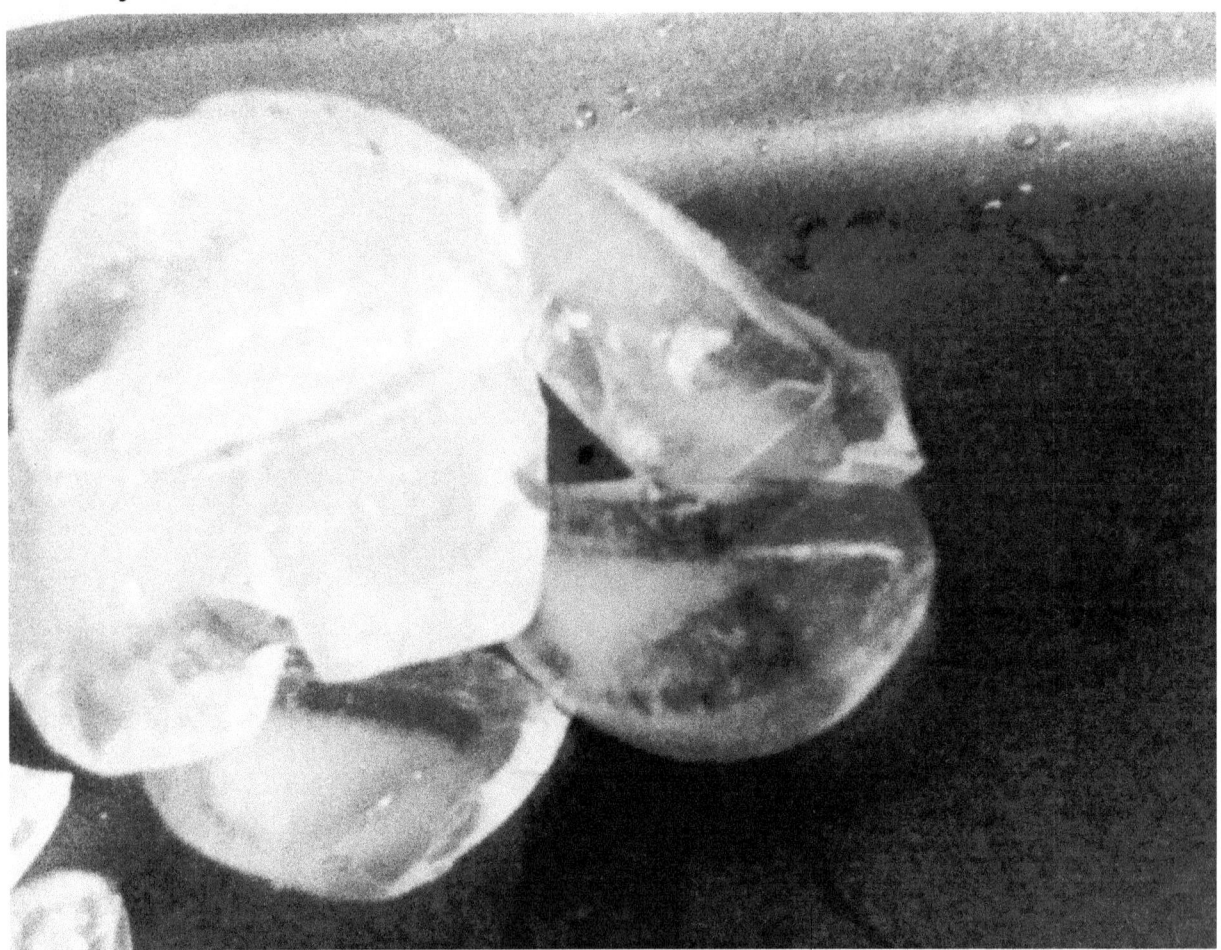

Ice cools and drips at what hot and wet about

Your love and sexy feelings. To make you feel sweet bitter

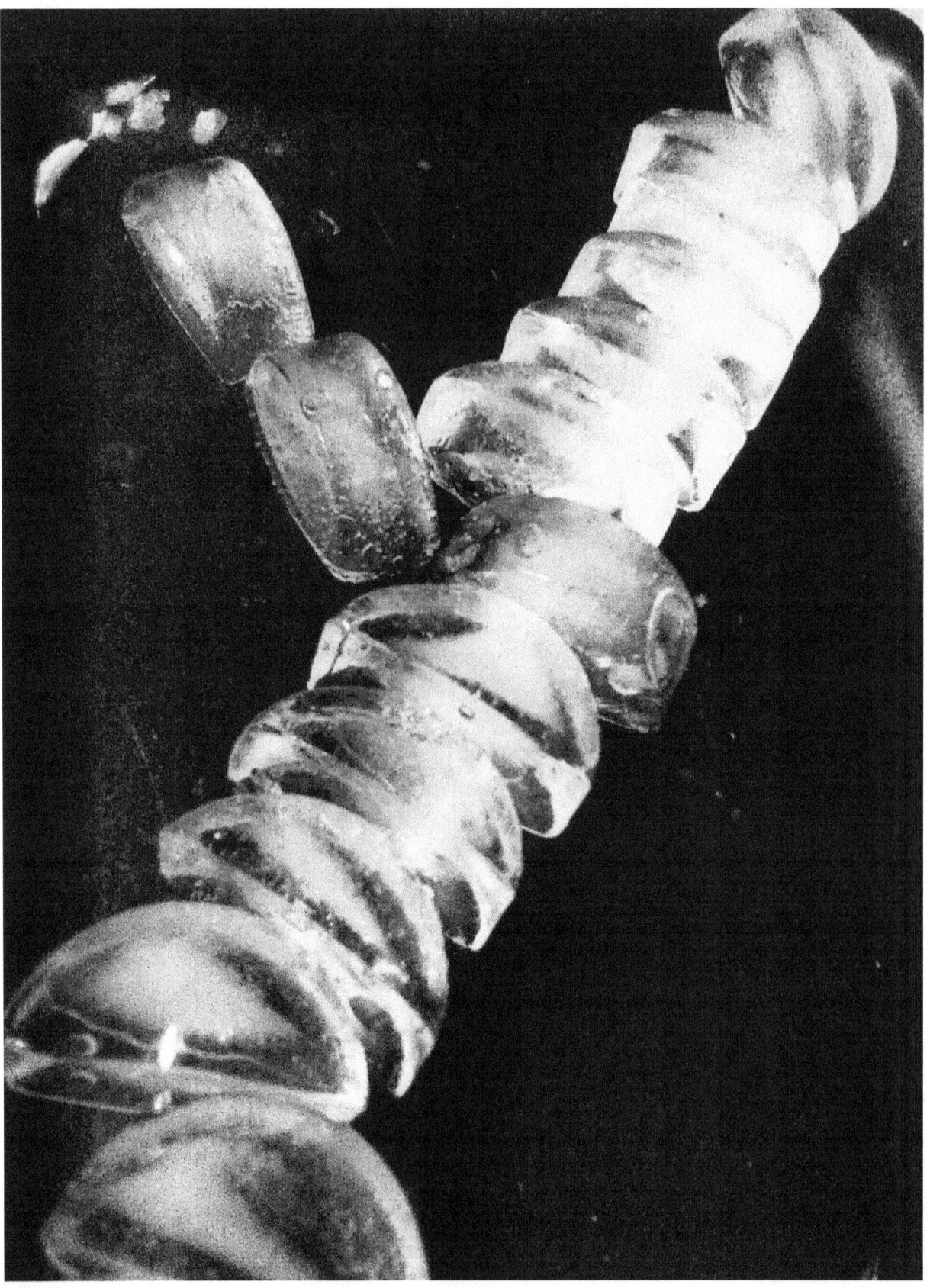

moments of passion
Just yelling each others
Name and loving it.

The ice becomes the tools of fantastic fantasy's.

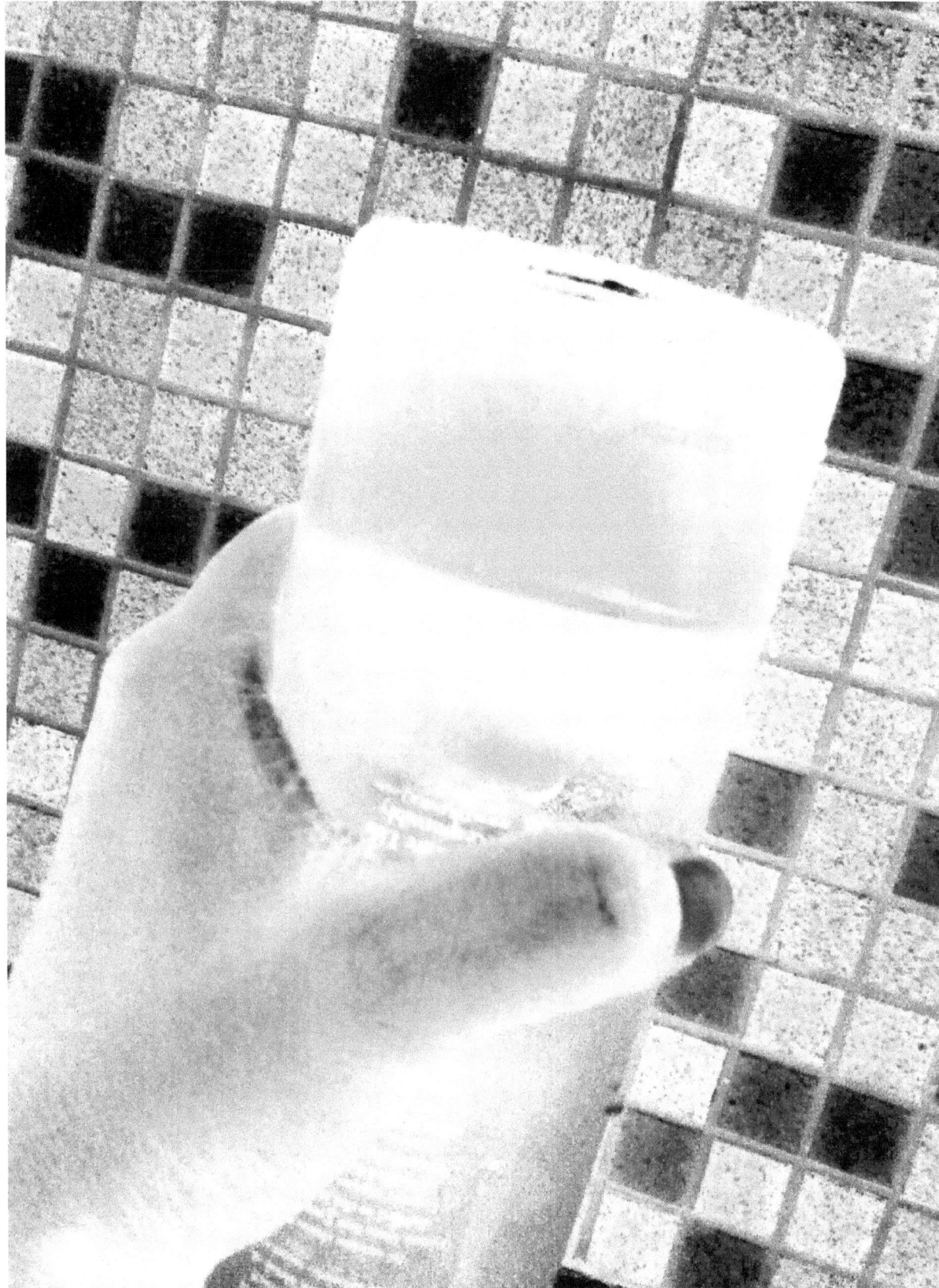

Cool your lips with a
Drink of whatever gives

You loving and true feelings of well you know I do not have to spell it out for you and your own relationships.

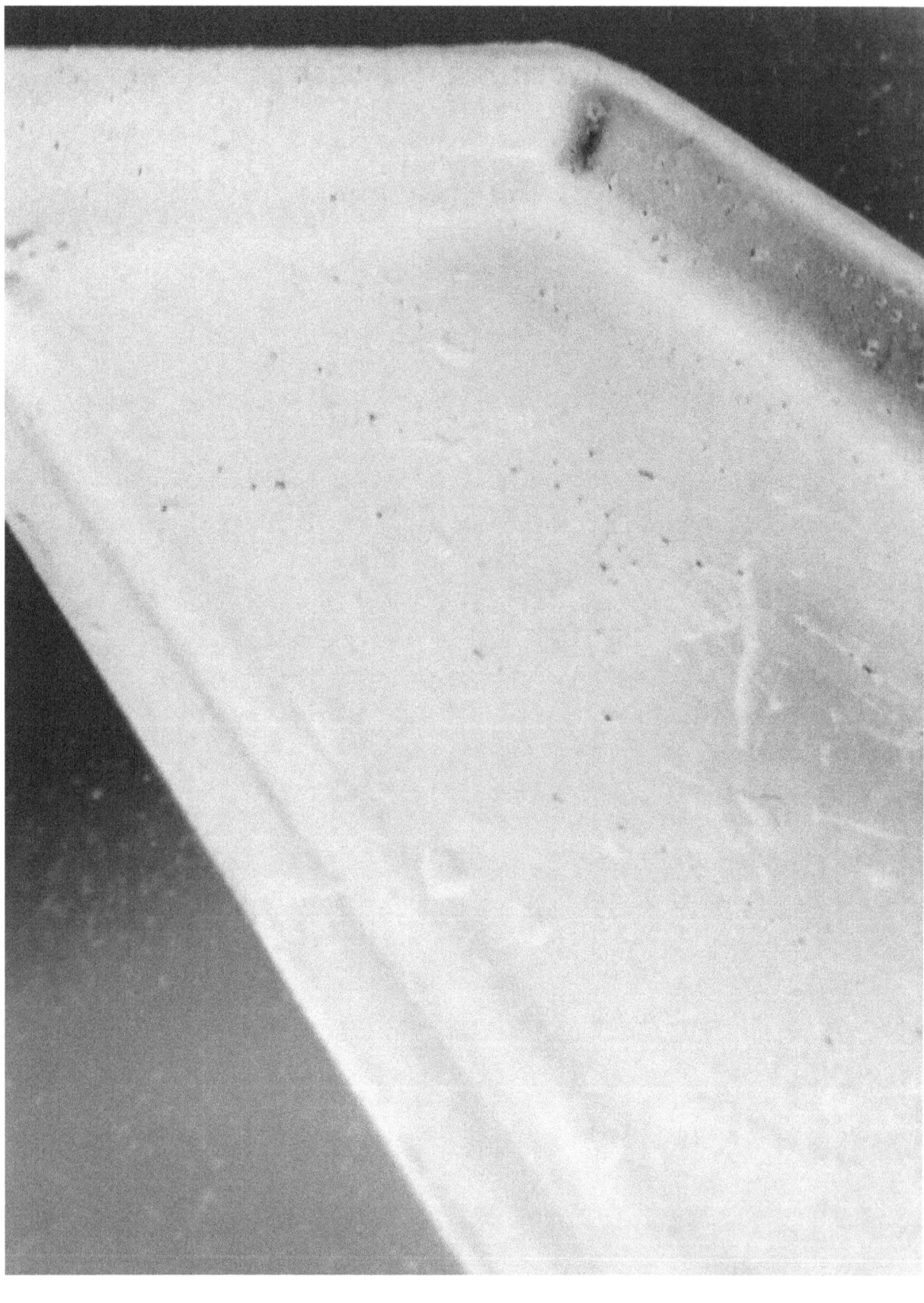

Then he is gone like this
Empty item in your life
For players are danger
But they do help you find
What you have been looking for all along.
A time of being treated
In diamonds and silk

Where someone shows

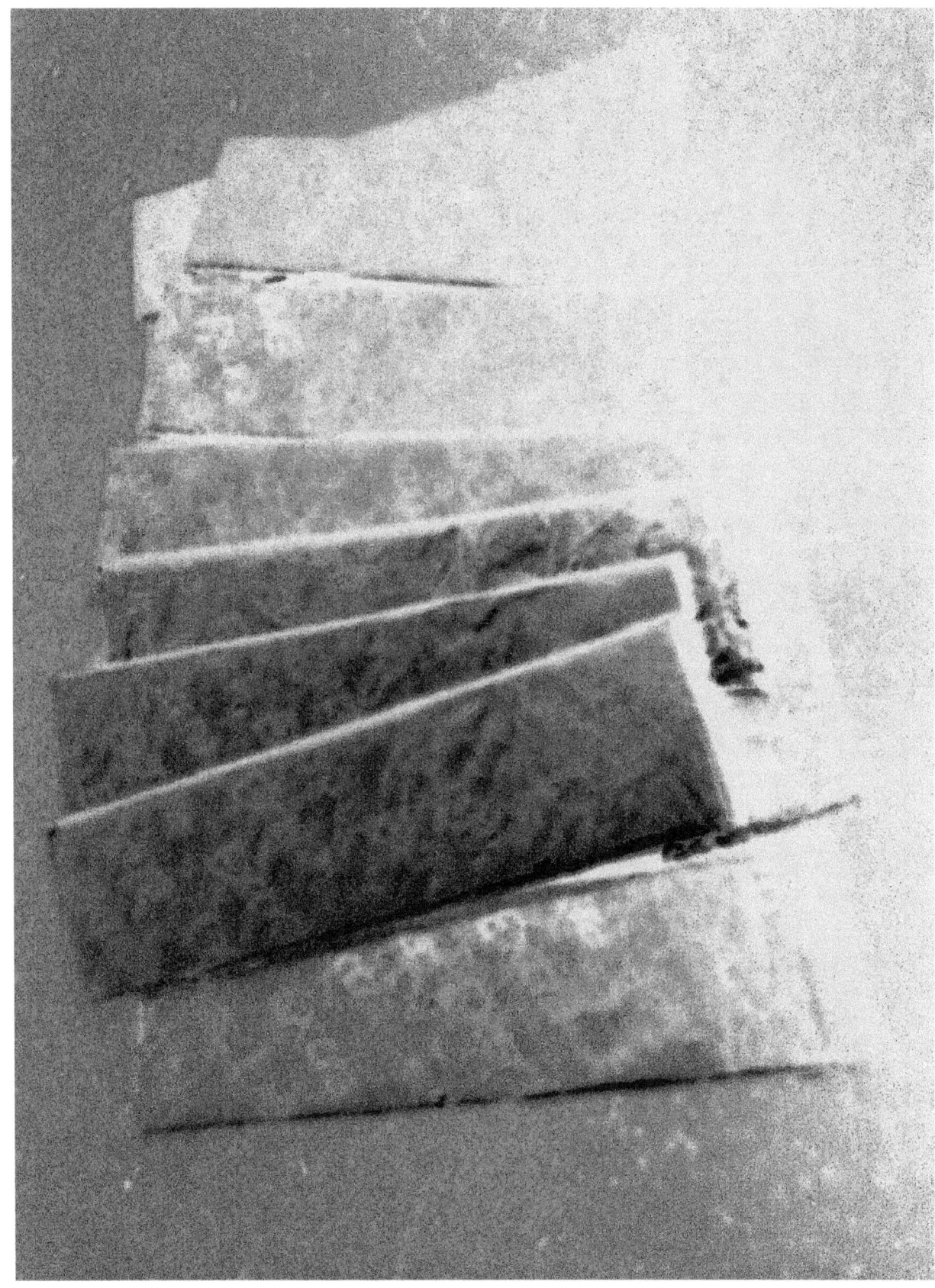

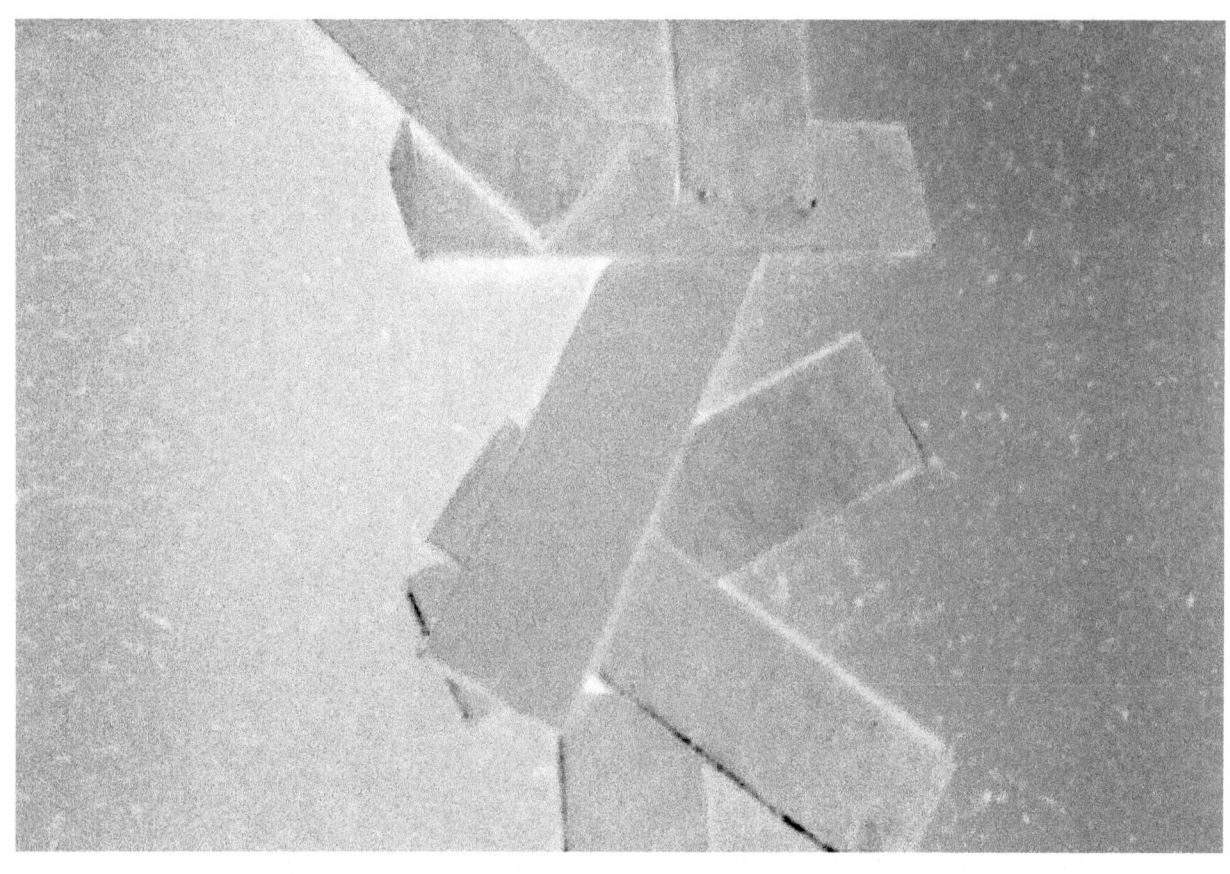

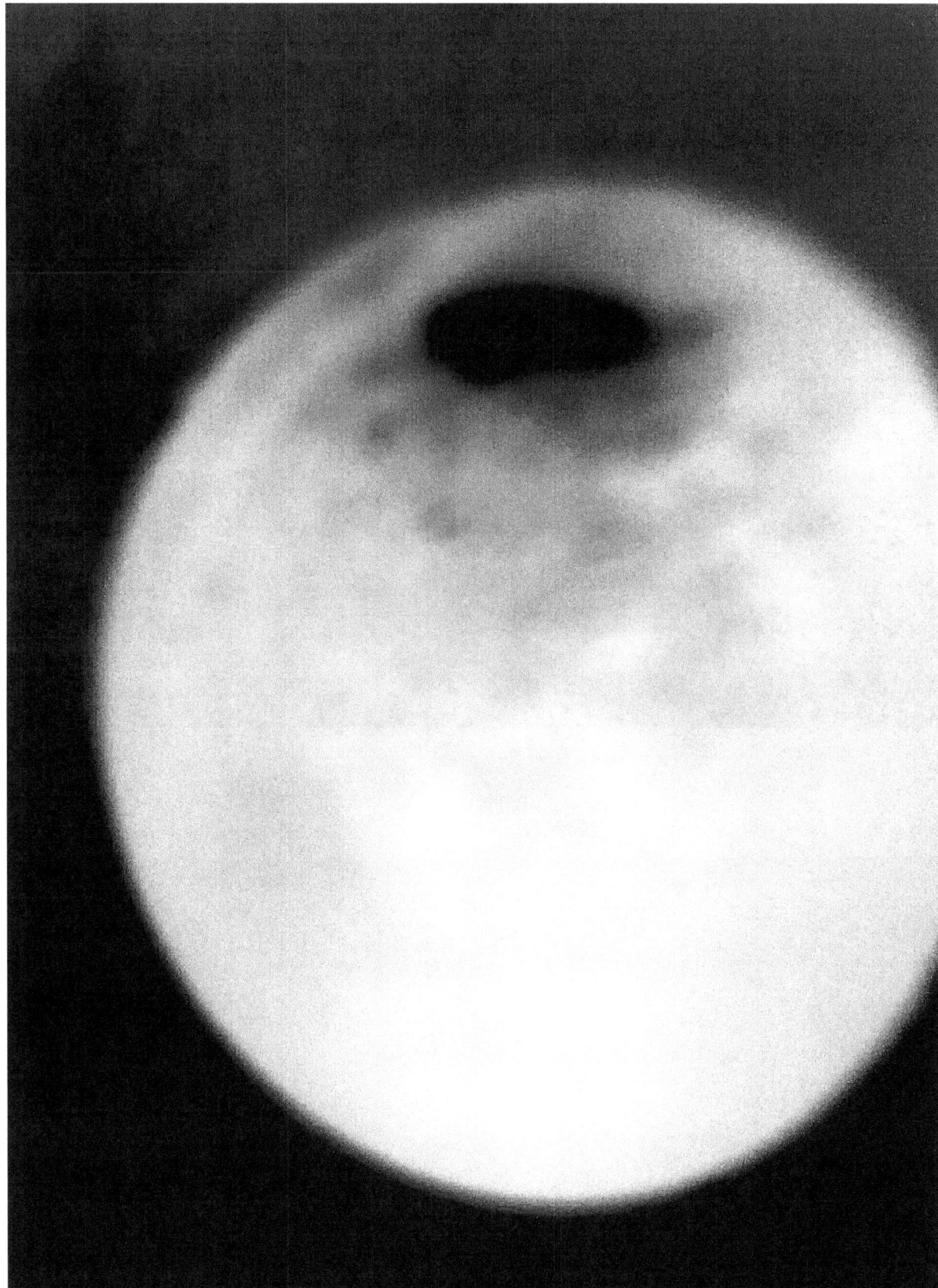

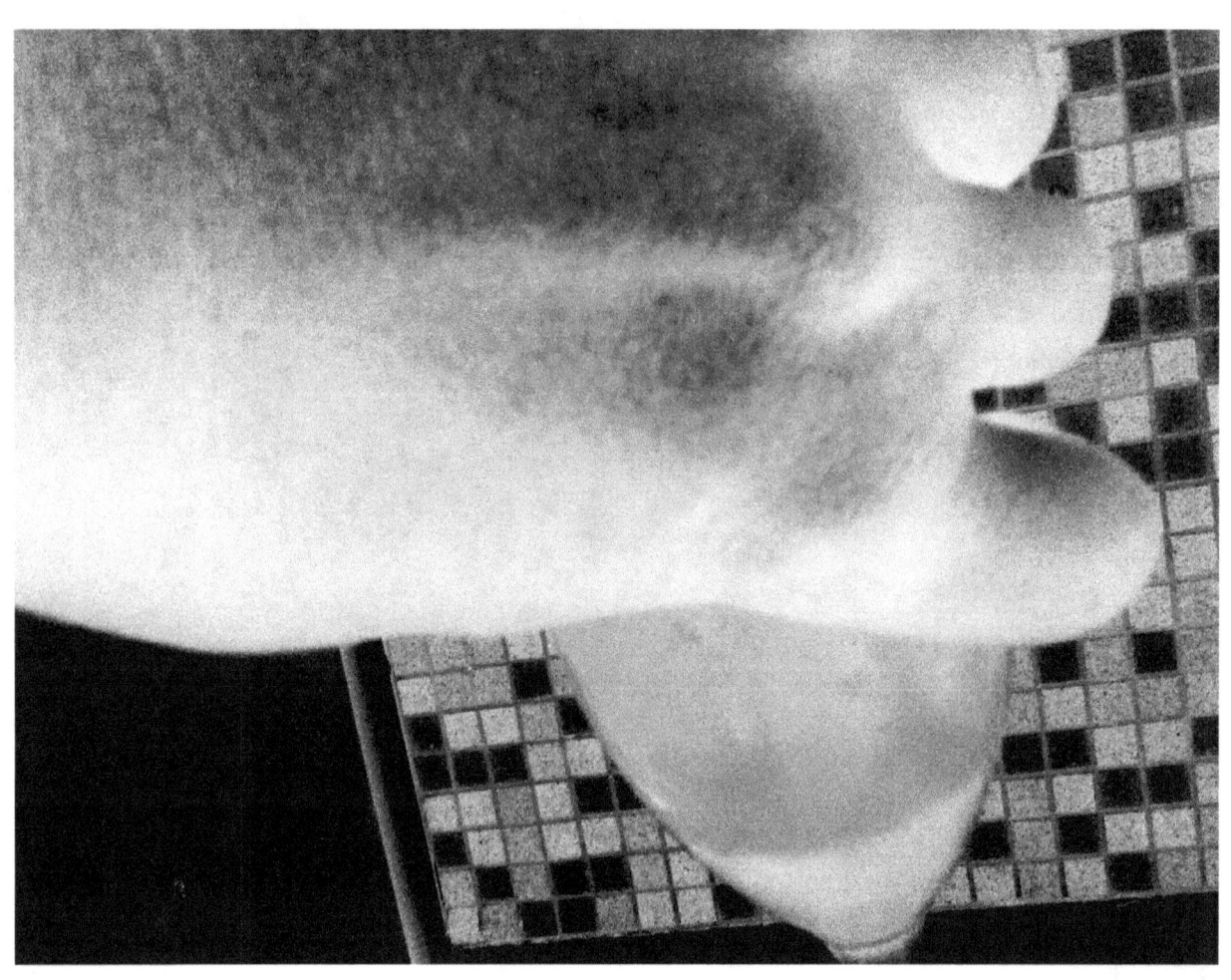

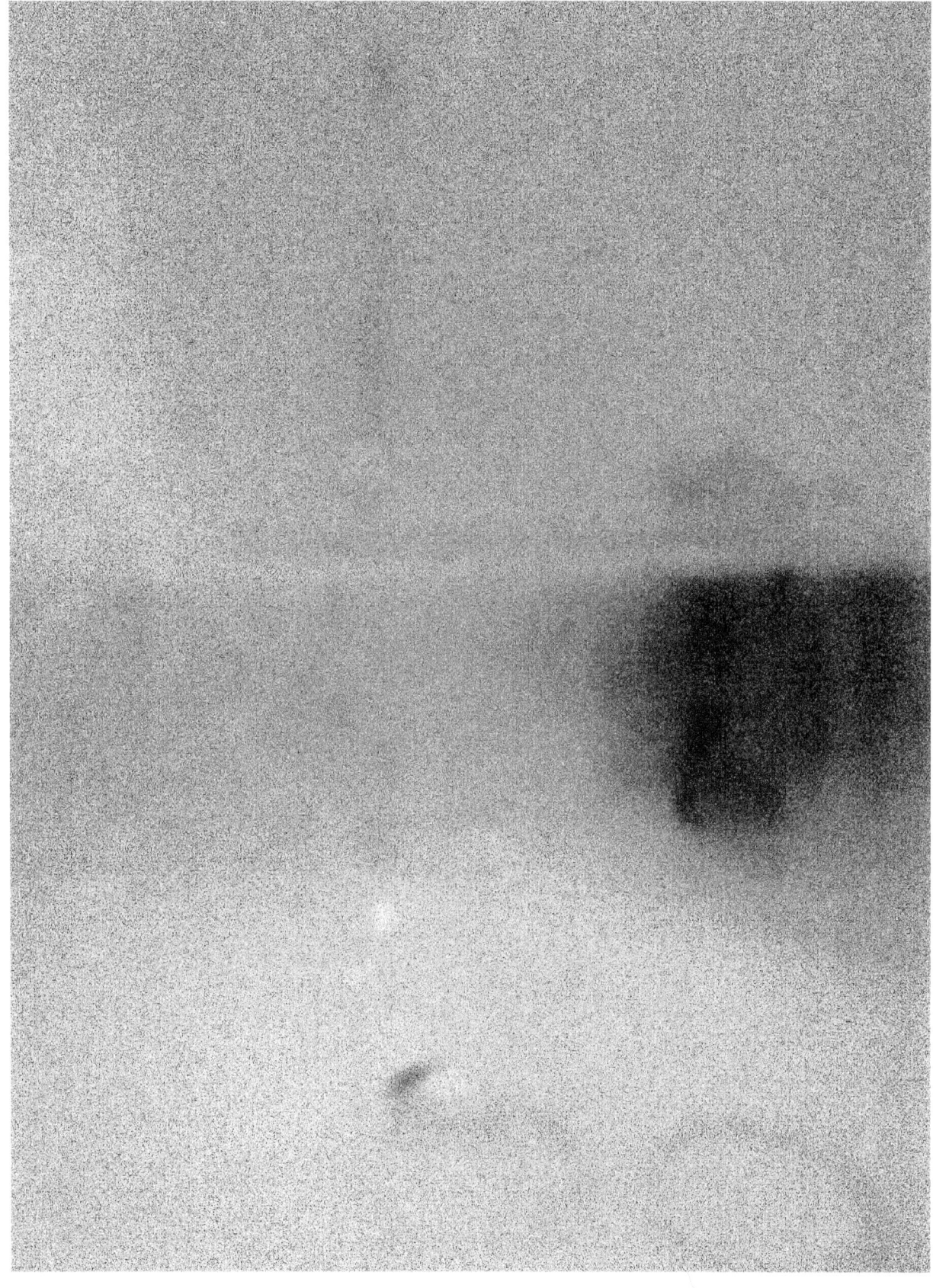

You what the meaning
Of love and the lovely
Side of life for a change
In to your string of candy
Melt gum which you can
Eat and enjoy for many times to come.

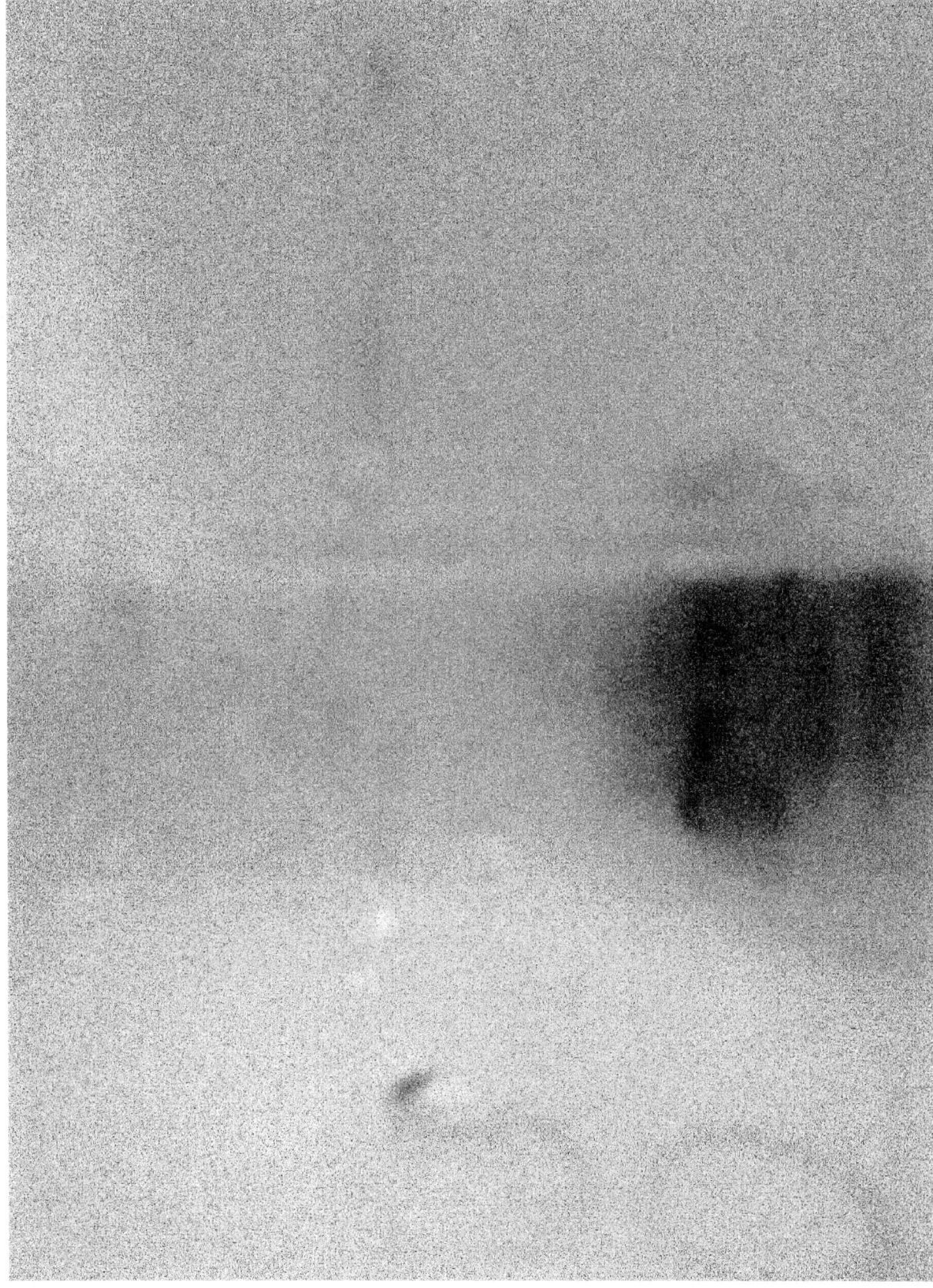

The heat and melting of this image is so sweet
You just never want to come out of loving a
Fantasy.

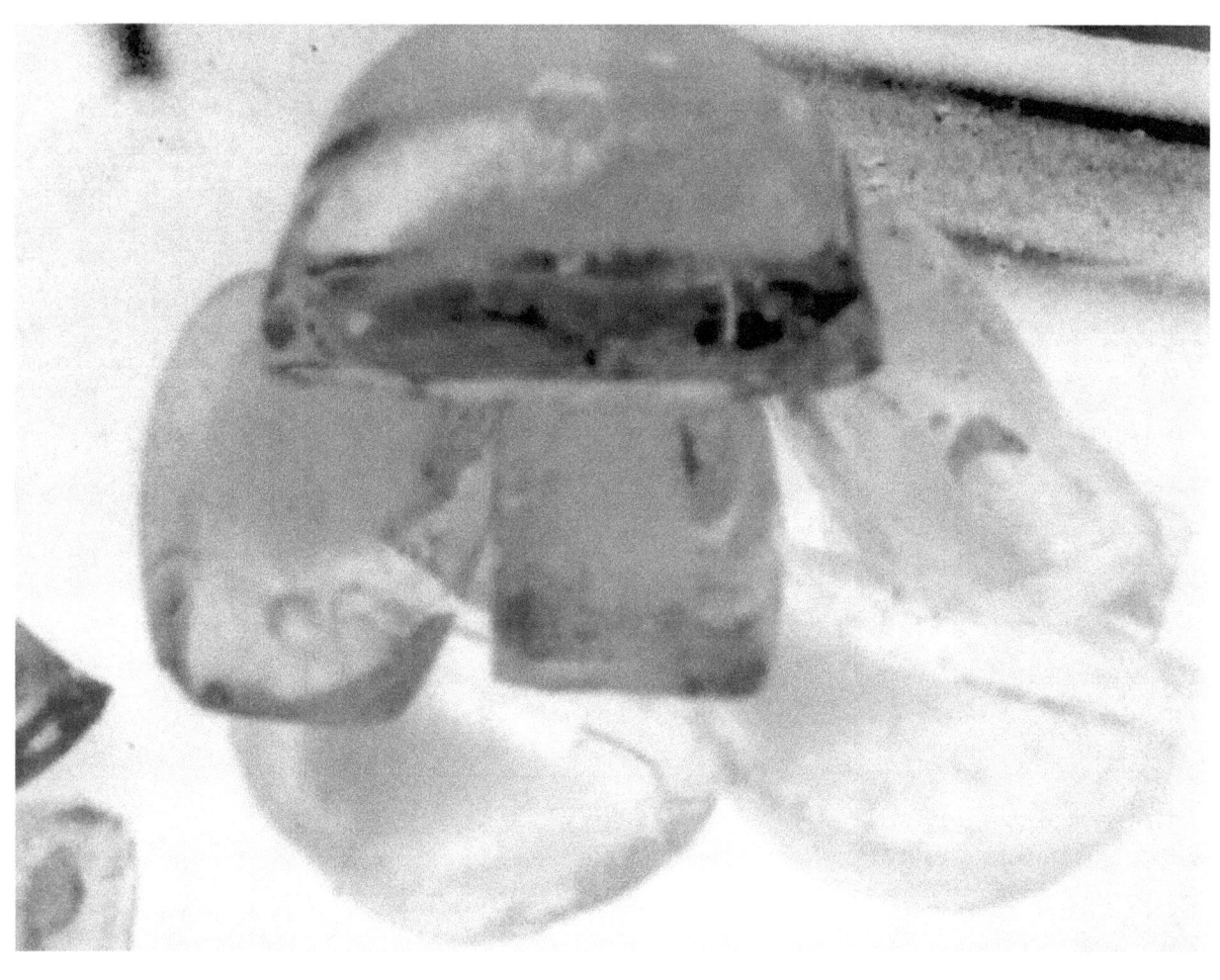

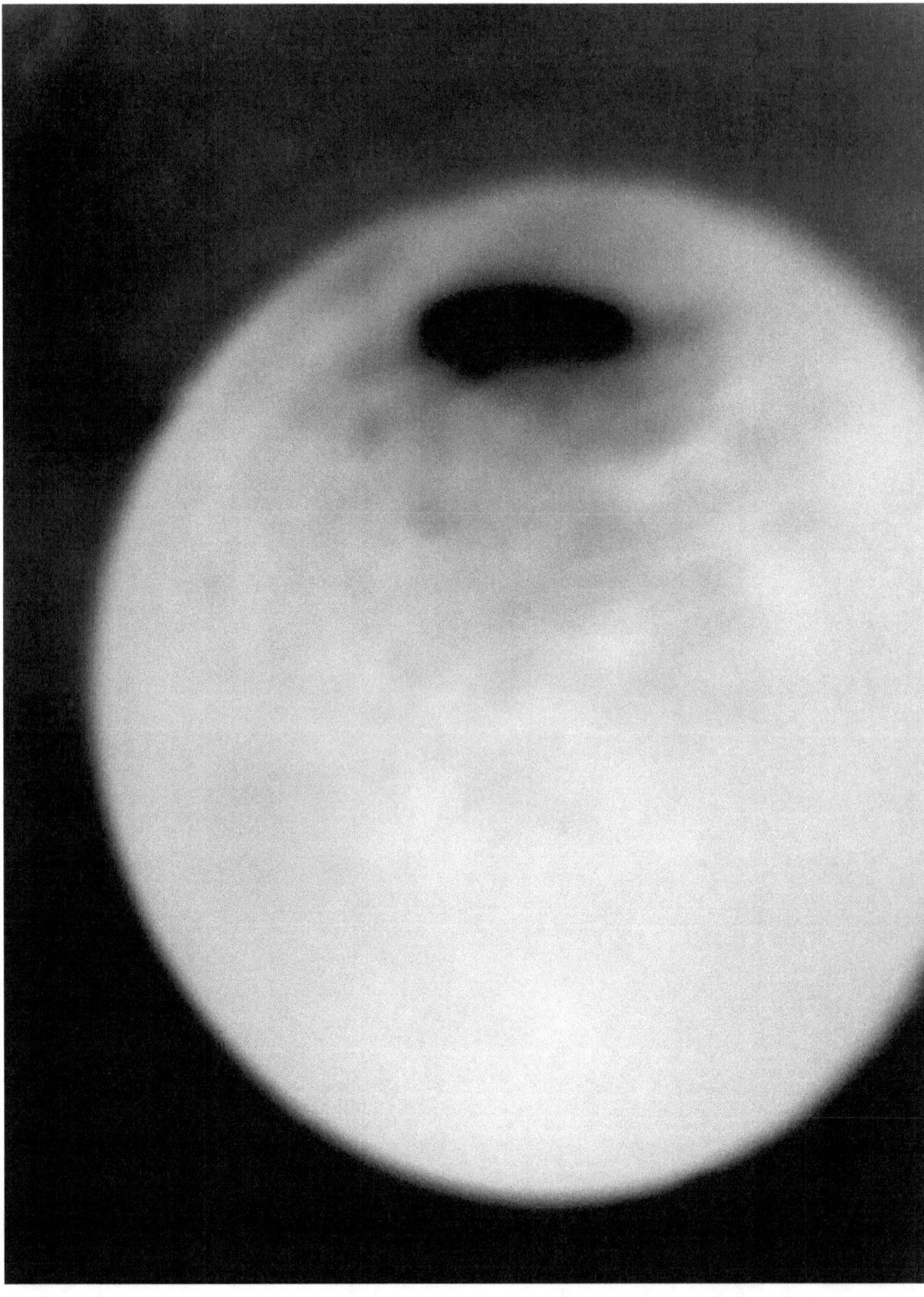

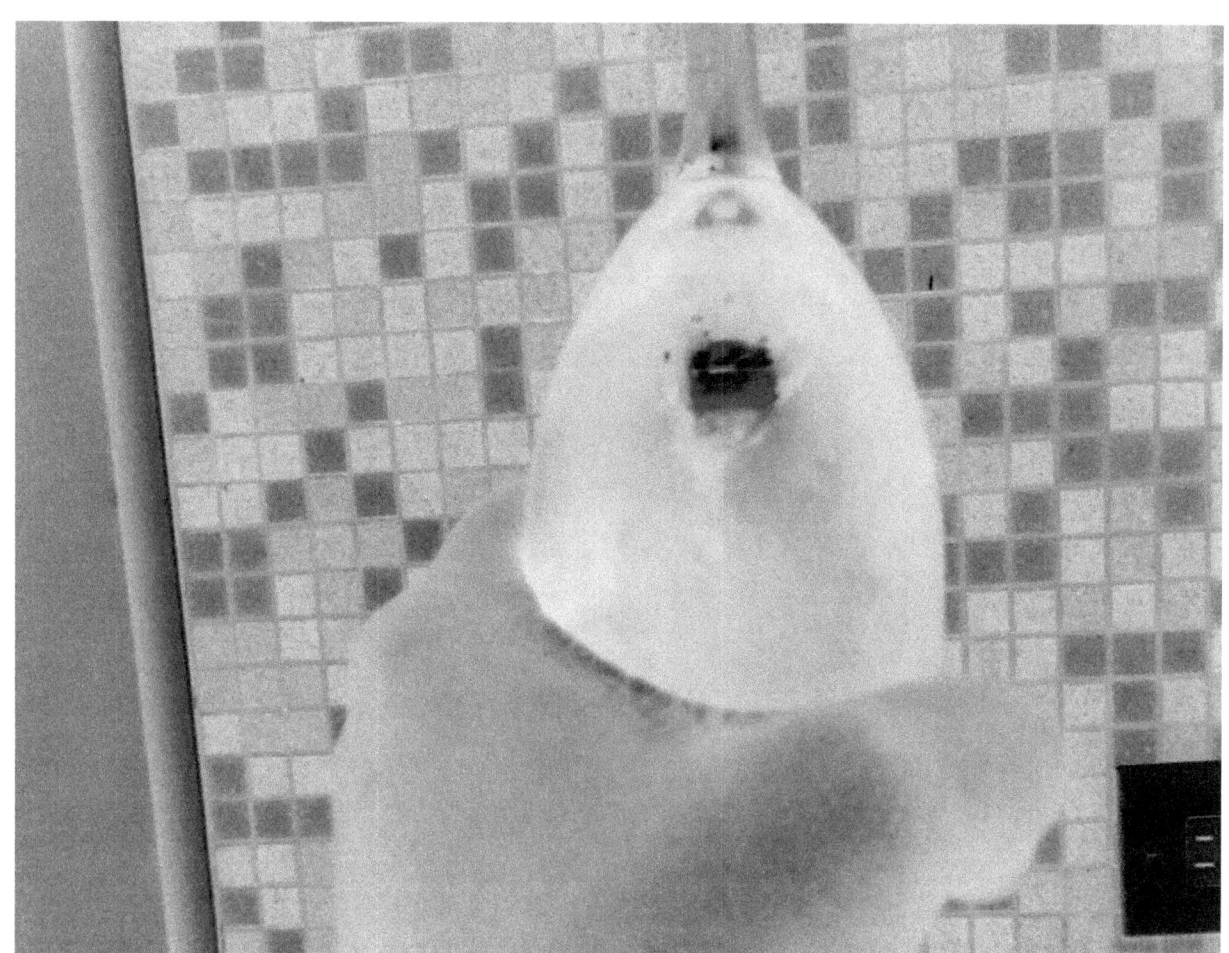

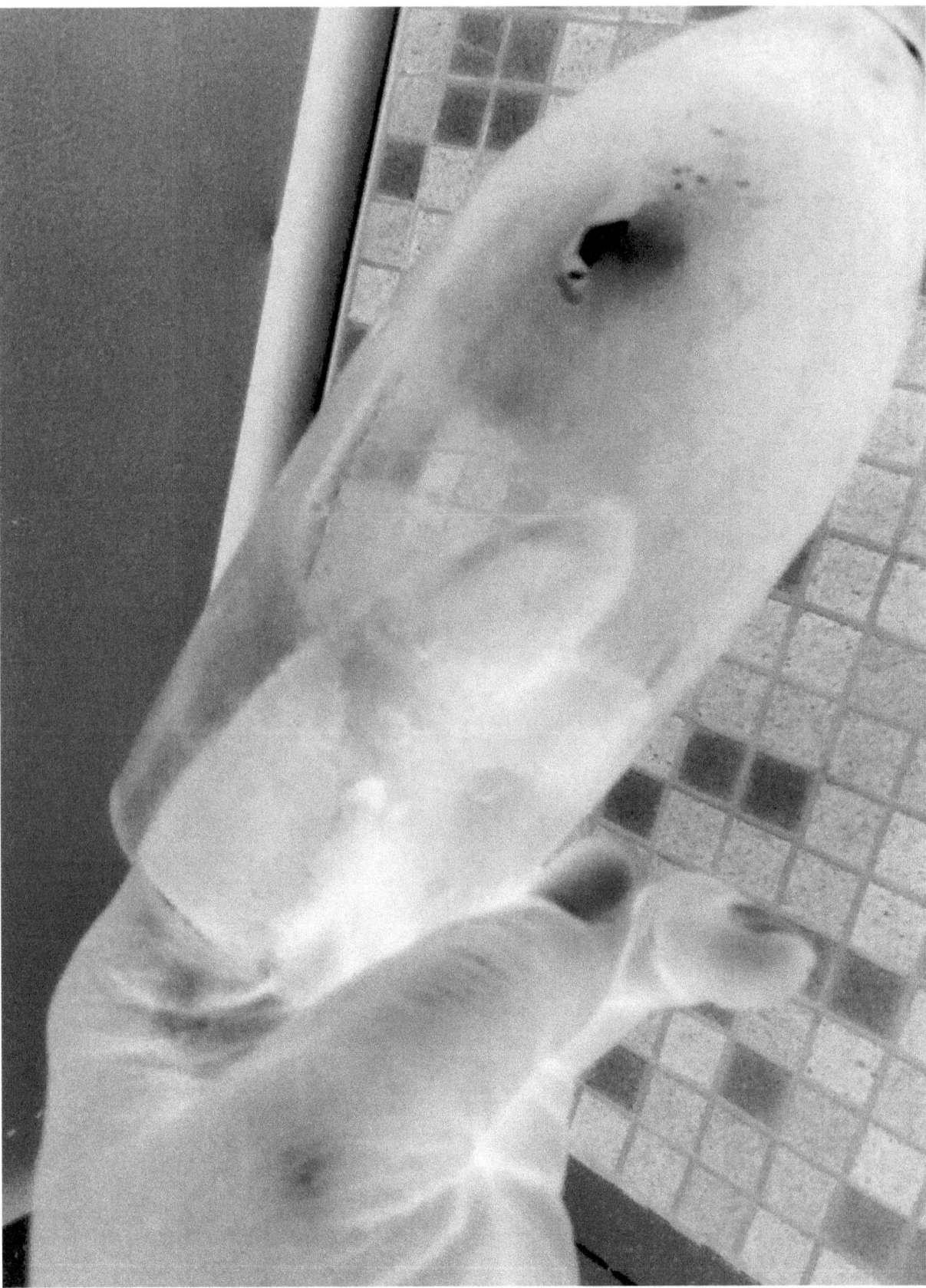

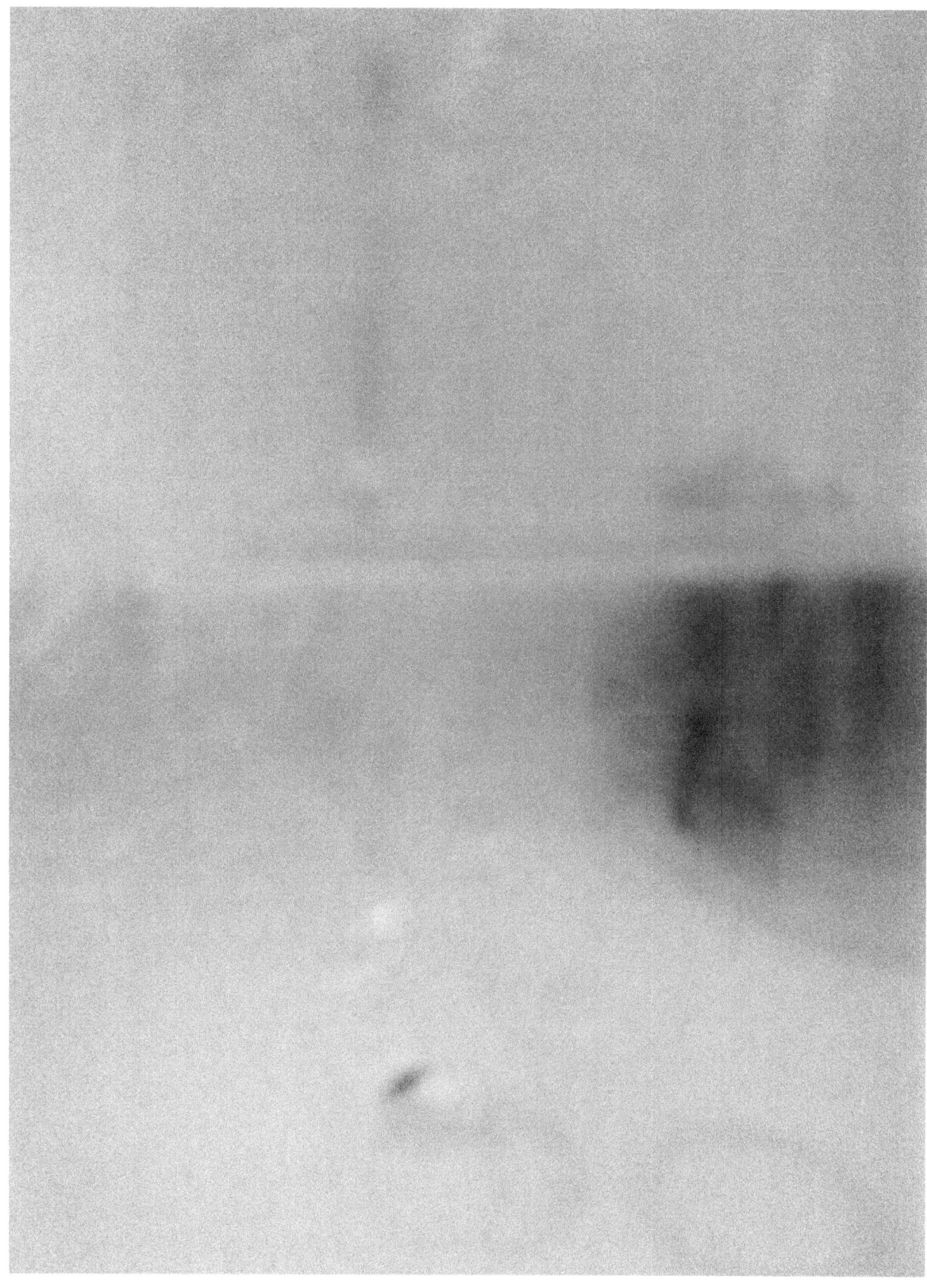

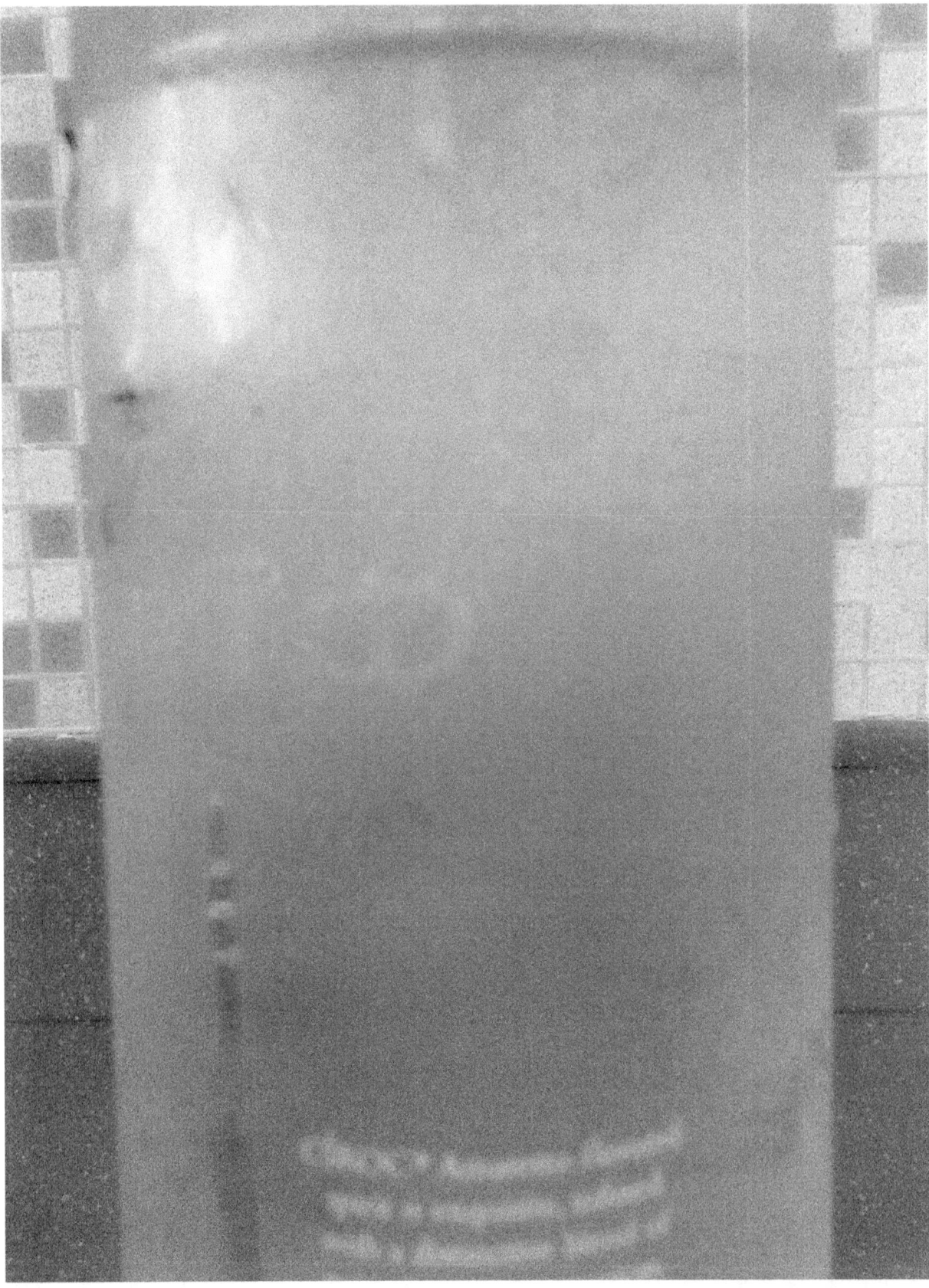

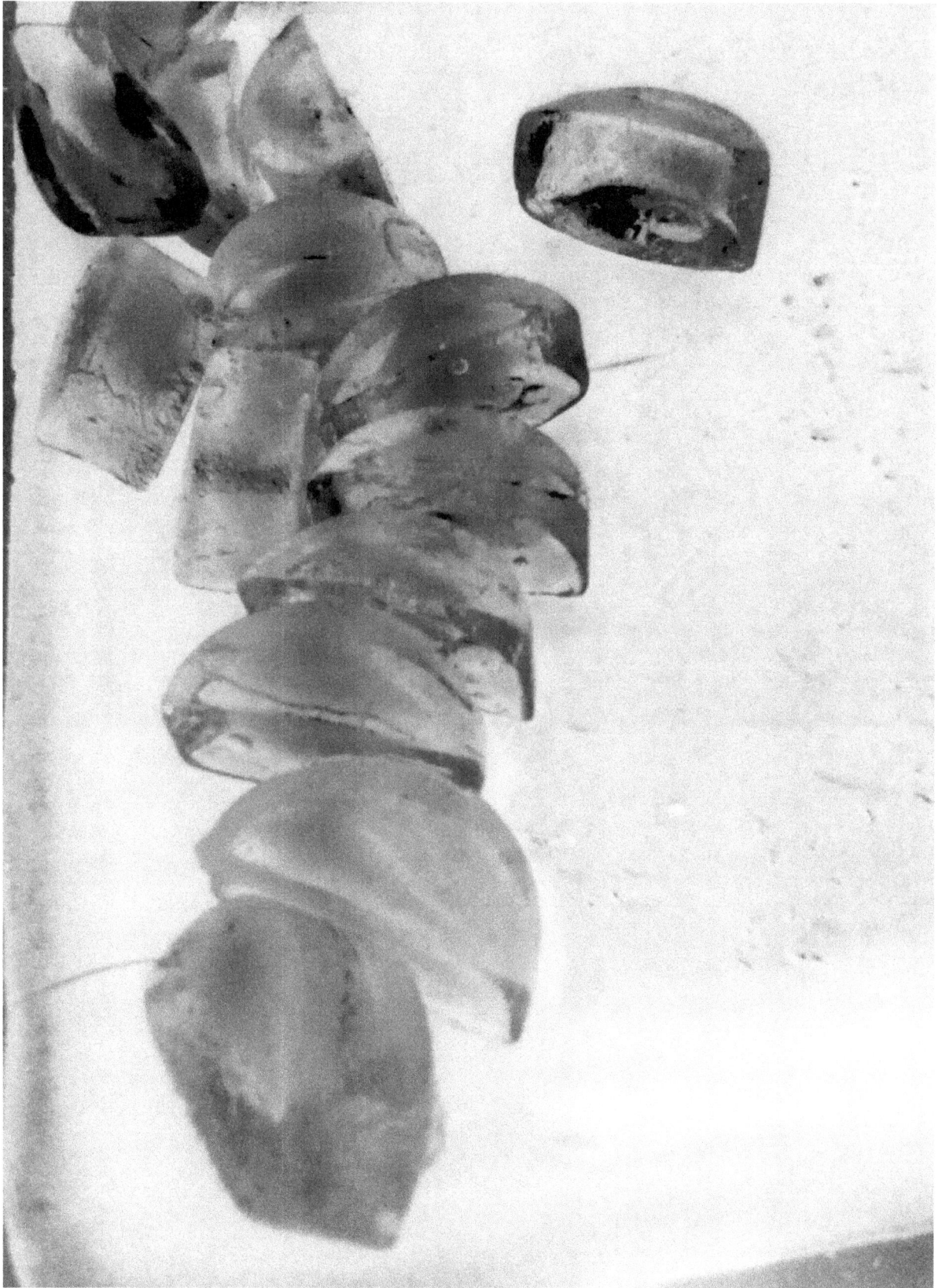

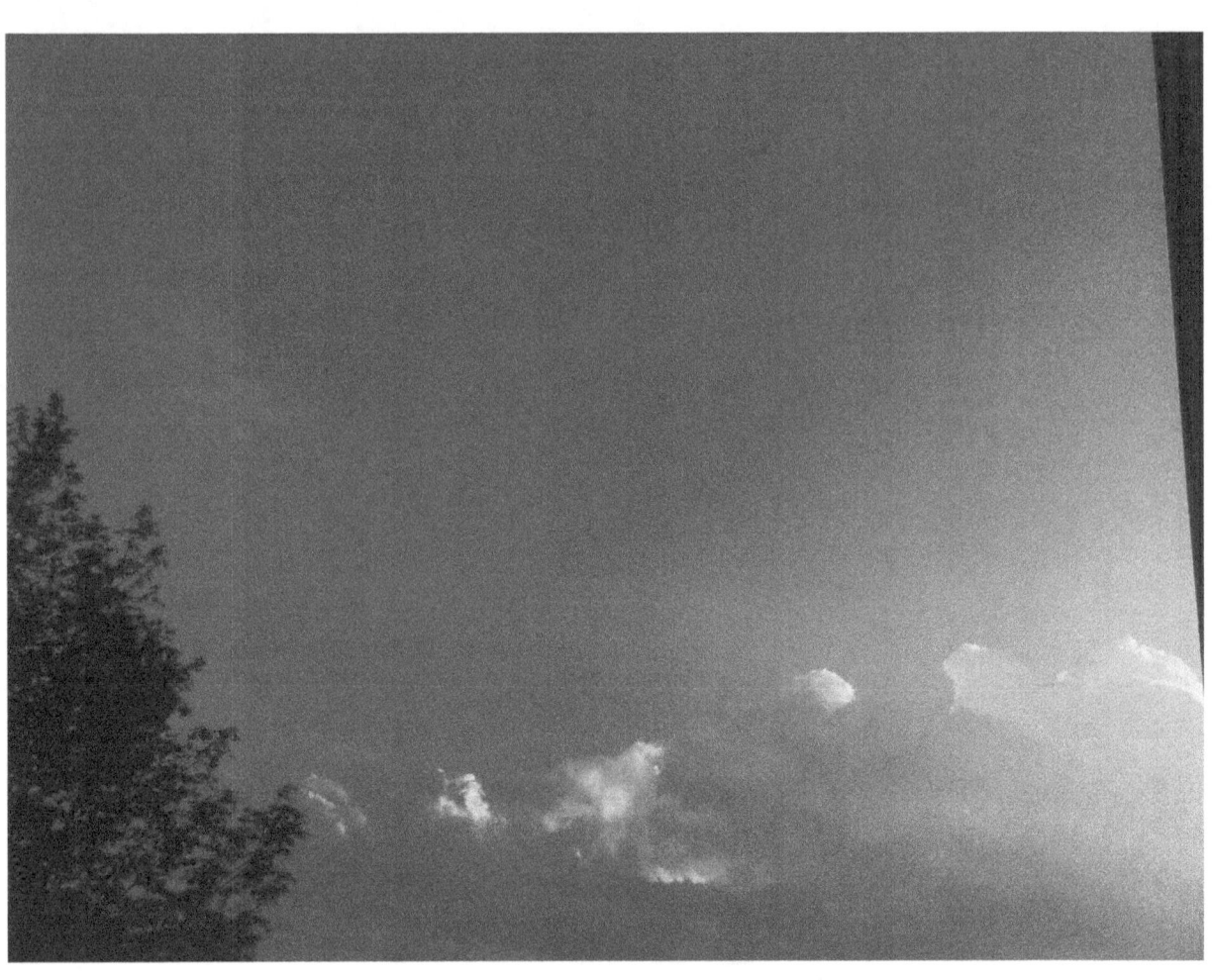

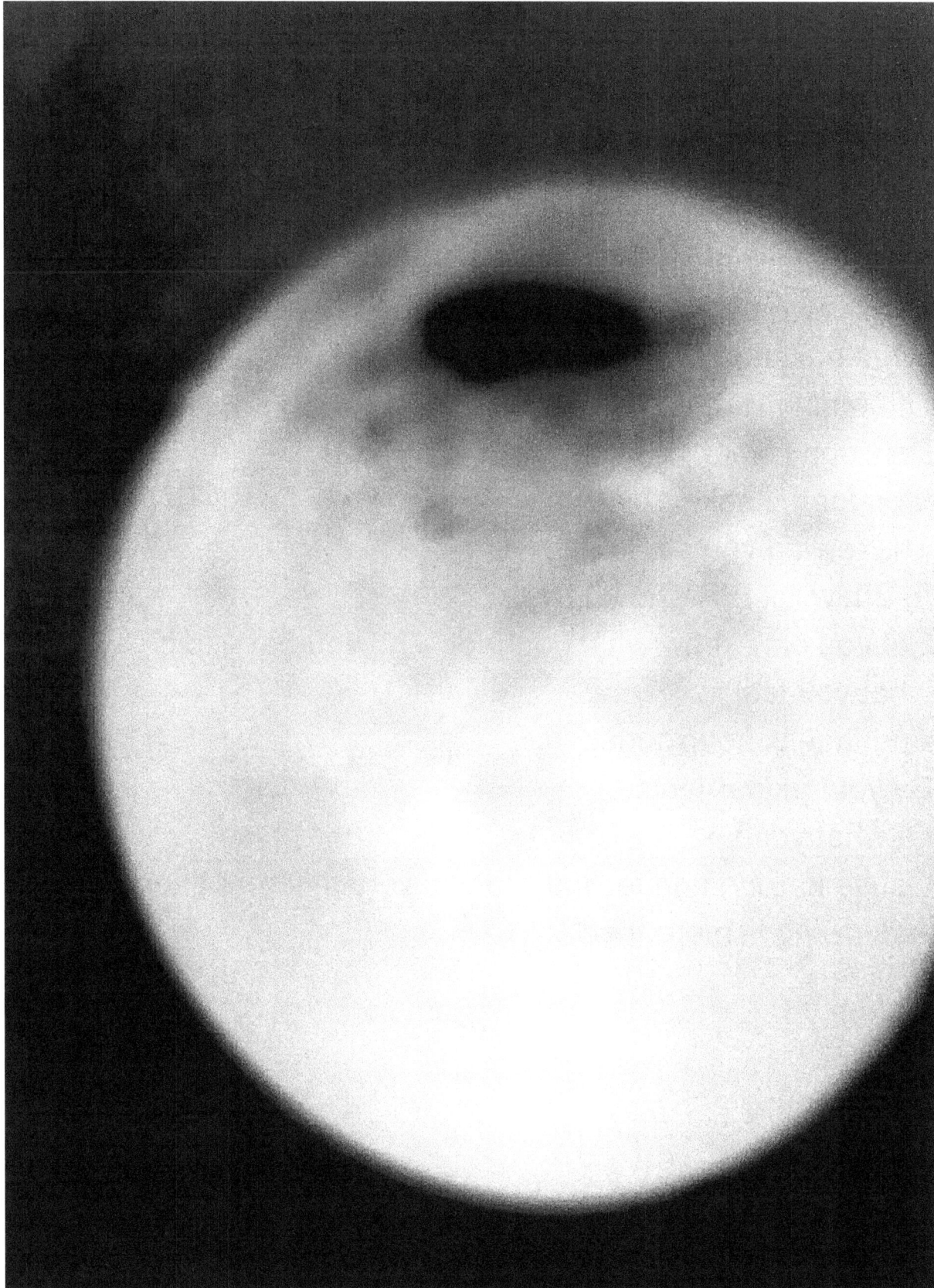

For when night hits at your love
Your soul dances with
Pleasure like no other.
Yes this is what I wanted
You to see art.
Meeting loving
And how we look at
What maybe a kiss
Of pouring waters
Between lovers poring
It on for the sake of
The feeling you get from
It. But will it last who knows.
But you only know what you feel. And you have to be sure of
what you feel.
And that its not clouded
By your judgements
Of what you see.
Cause looking and feeling are two very different things
And loving is more then

These to emotions.

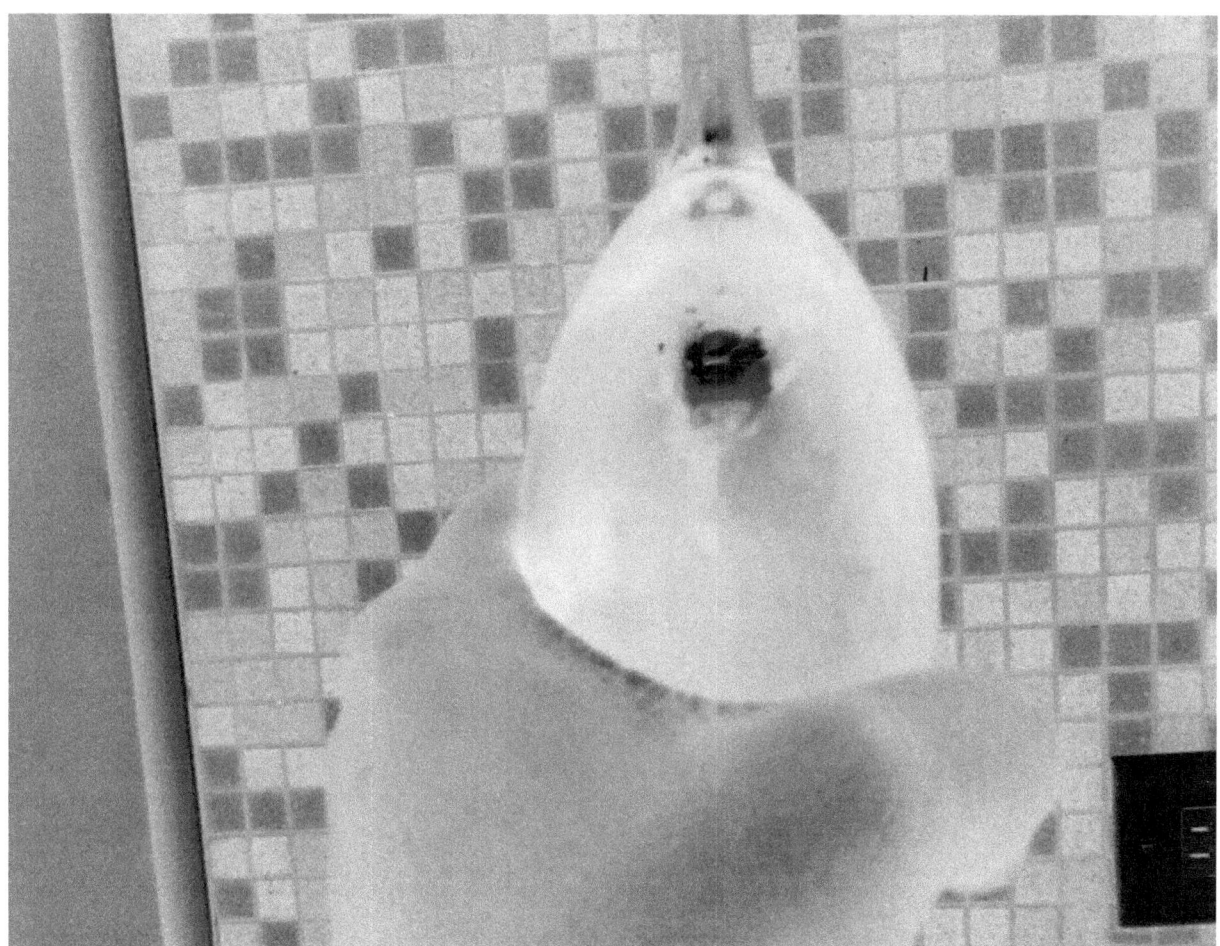

If you don't get what you want
You may try to brake
The wine glass you love
But don't hurt the other
Parties involved cause

You can always find another in love you know.

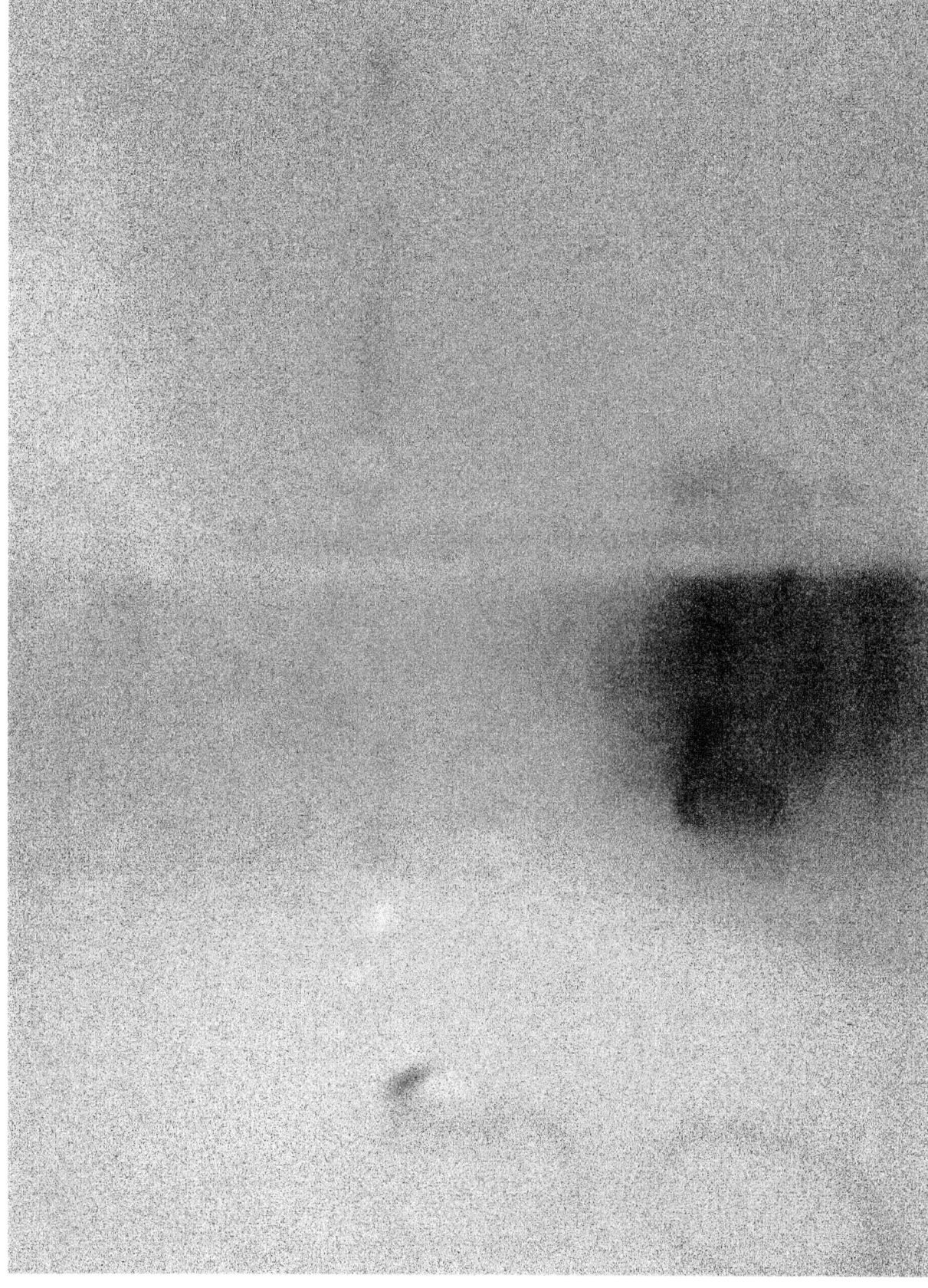

On a hot steamy day
Or if its raining you
See the glass outside become a blurred wet
Thing which you can't
See clearly out of it
Anymore. So look carefully at what is before you
Make your own mind up
About it
And proceed with love
So it will turn into
Loving.

Chapter 7

Yes this where we go
When its to hot to handle.
But it can be so good
When its like that.
For keep a level head
And make sure you
Are enjoying what is at
Your table
To well you know.

Roll That Cigar

We in that time and moment
You at my table
And I am thinking
Wow what brings you to
Me. Then I realize it
Was the motion of how
I moved at you when you started talking to
Me
That's what feels good you know like a cigar in
My fingers as I am rolling it for the mass out there.
What gets me through is I think of this product as.you.

www.ingramcontent.com/pod-product-compliance
Lightning Source LLC
Chambersburg PA
CBHW080716190526
45169CB00006B/2394